New York Academic Content Standards

Standard 1 Social Studies: History of the United States and New York

Students will: use a variety of intellectual skills to demonstrate their understanding of major ideas, eras, themes, developments, and turning points in the history of the United States and New York.

1.1 The study of New York State and United States history requires an analysis of the development of American culture, its diversity and multicultural context, and the ways people are unified by many values, practices, and traditions.

1.2 Important ideas, social and cultural values, beliefs, and traditions from New York State and United States history illustrate the connections and interactions of people and events across time and from a variety of perspectives.

1.3 Study about the major social, political, economic, cultural, and religious developments in New York State and United States history involves learning about the important roles and contributions of individuals and groups.

1.4 The skills of historical analysis include the ability to: explain the significance of historical evidence; weigh the importance, reliability, and validity of evidence; understand the concept of multiple causation; understand the importance of changing and competing interpretations of different historical developments.

Standard 2 Social Studies: World History

Students will: use a variety of intellectual skills to demonstrate their understanding of major ideas, eras, themes, developments, and turning points in world history and examine the broad sweep of history from a variety of perspectives.

2.1 The study of world history requires an understanding of world cultures and civilizations, including an analysis of important ideas, social and cultural values, beliefs, and traditions. This study also examines the human condition and the connections and interactions of people across time and space and the ways different people view the same event or issue from a variety of perspectives.

2.2 Establishing timeframes, exploring different periodizations, examining themes across time and within cultures, and focusing on important turning points in world history help organize the study of world cultures and civilizations.

2.3 Study of the major social, political, cultural, and religious developments in world history involves learning about the important roles and contributions of individuals and groups.

2.4 The skills of historical analysis include the ability to investigate differing and competing interpretations of the theories of history, hypothesize about why interpretations change over time, explain the importance of historical evidence, and understand the concepts of change and continuity over time.

Standard 3 Social Studies: Geography
Students will: use a variety of intellectual skills to demonstrate their understanding of the geography of the interdependent world in which we live—local, national, and global—including the distribution of people, places, and environments over the Earth's surface.

3.1 Geography can be divided into six essential elements which can be used to analyze important historic, geographic, economic, and environmental questions and issues. These six elements include: the world in spatial terms, places and regions, physical settings (including natural resources), human systems, environment and society, and the use of geography. (Adapted from The National Geography Standards, 1994: Geography for Life)

3.2 Geography requires the development and application of the skills of asking and answering geographic questions; analyzing theories of geography; and acquiring, organizing, and analyzing geographic information. (Adapted from: The National Geography Standards, 1994: Geography for Life)

Standard 4 Social Studies: Economics
Students will: use a variety of intellectual skills to demonstrate their understanding of how the United States and other societies develop economic systems and associated institutions to allocate scarce resources, how major decision-making units function in the U.S. and other national economies, and how an economy solves the scarcity problem through market and nonmarket mechanisms.

4.1 The study of economics requires an understanding of major economic concepts and systems, the principles of economic decision making, and the interdependence of economies and economic systems throughout the world.

4.2 Economics requires the development and application of the skills needed to make informed and well-reasoned economic decisions in daily and national life.

Standard 5 Social Studies: Civics, Citizenship, and Government
Students will: use a variety of intellectual skills to demonstrate their understanding of the necessity for establishing governments; the governmental system of the U.S. and other nations; the U.S. Constitution; the basic civic values of American constitutional democracy; and the roles, rights, and responsibilities of citizenship, including avenues of participation.

5.1 The study of civics, citizenship, and government involves learning about political systems; the purposes of government and civic life; and the differing assumptions held by people across time and place regarding power, authority, governance, and law. (Adapted from The National Standards for Civics and Government, 1994)

5.2 The state and federal governments established by the Constitutions of the United States and the State of New York embody basic civic values (such as justice, honesty, self-discipline, due process, equality, majority rule with respect for minority rights, and respect for self, others, and property), principles, and practices and establish a system of shared and limited government. (Adapted from The National Standards for Civics and Government, 1994)

5.3 Central to civics and citizenship is an understanding of the roles of the citizen within American constitutional democracy and the scope of a citizen's rights and responsibilities.

5.4 The study of civics and citizenship requires the ability to probe ideas and assumptions, ask and answer analytical questions, take a skeptical attitude toward questionable arguments, evaluate evidence, formulate rational conclusions, and develop and refine participatory skills.

NEW YORK

Macmillan/McGraw-Hill **TIMELINKS**

The United States, Canada, and Latin America

PROGRAM AUTHORS

James A. Banks
Kevin P. Colleary
Linda Greenow
Walter C. Parker
Emily M. Schell
Dinah Zike

CONTRIBUTORS

Raymond C. Jones
Irma M. Olmedo

 Macmillan/McGraw-Hill

Volume I

PROGRAM AUTHORS

James A. Banks, Ph.D.
Kerry and Linda Killinger
  Professor of Diversity Studies
  and Director, Center for
  Multicultural Education
University of Washington
Seattle, Washington

Kevin P. Colleary, Ed.D.
Curriculum and Teaching Department
Graduate School of Education
Fordham University
New York, New York

Linda Greenow, Ph.D.
Associate Professor and Chair
Department of Geography
State University of New York at
  New Paltz
New Paltz, New York

Walter C. Parker, Ph.D.
Professor of Social Studies Education,
University of Washington
Seattle, Washington

Emily M. Schell, Ed.D.
Visiting Professor, Teacher Education
San Diego State University
San Diego, California

Dinah Zike
Educational Consultant
Dinah-Mite Activities, Inc.
San Antonio, Texas

CONTRIBUTORS

Raymond C. Jones, Ph.D.
Director of Secondary Social Studies
  Education
Wake Forest University
Winston-Salem, North Carolina

Irma M. Olmedo
Associate Professor
University of Illinois-Chicago
College of Education
Chicago, Illinois

HISTORIANS/SCHOLARS

Manuel Chavez, Ph.D.
Associate Director, Center for Latin
  American & Caribbean Studies,
  Assistant Professor, School of
  Journalism
Michigan State University
East Lansing, Michigan

Lawrence Dale, Ph.D.
Director, Center for Economic
  Education
Arkansas State University
Jonesboro, Arkansas

Brooks Green, Ph.D.
Professor of Geography
University of Central Arkansas
Conway, Arkansas

Jason R. Young, Ph.D.
Assistant Professor of History
SUNY, Buffalo
Buffalo, New York

GRADE LEVEL REVIEWERS

Diane Downer
Fifth Grade Teacher
Monica B. Leary Elementary
Rush, New York

Judith Kapila
Fifth Grade Teacher
PS #16 Troy City Schools
Troy, New York

Kim Pittsley
Fifth Grade Teacher
Commack Road Elementary School
Islip, New York

Jennifer Tomm, NBCT
Lead Elementary Social Studies
  Teacher
Rochester City School District
Rochester, New York

learning through listening

Students with print disabilities may be eligible to obtain an accessible, audio version of the pupil edition of this textbook. Please call Recording for the Blind & Dyslexic at 1-800-221-4792 for complete information.

The McGraw·Hill Companies

Macmillan McGraw-Hill

Send all inquires to:

Macmillan/McGraw-Hill
8787 Orion Place
Columbus, OH 43240-4027

MHID 0-02-152299-5

ISBN 978-0-02-152299-6

Printed in the United States of America.

2 3 4 5 6 7 8 9 10   027/043   13 12 11 10 09

The United States, Canada, and Latin America

CONTENTS, Volume 1

Unit 2 United States and Canada: From Past to Present

Reference Section

Skills and Features

Maps

Geography of the United States and Canada

Niagara Falls, Ontario, Canada

Unit 1

EXPLORE The Big Idea

Essential Question
How do people adapt to where they live?

FOLDABLES Study Organizer
Compare and Contrast
Make and label a two-tab book Foldable before you read Unit 1. Write: **Ways people change their environment** on the top tab. On the bottom tab write: **Ways people are affected by their environment**. Use the Foldable to organize information as you read.

Ways people change their environment

Ways people are affected by their environment

LOG ON
For more about the geography of the United States and Canada go to
www.macmillanmh.com

PEOPLE, PLACES, and EVENTS

John Wesley Powell

John Muir

Grand Canyon

1869
Powell explores the Grand Canyon

Yosemite

1890
Muir helps make Yosemite a national park

1865   1885   1905   1925

Powell led an expedition down the Green and Colorado rivers that included the first passage through the **Grand Canyon**.

Today you can see the Grand Canyon, one of the natural wonders of the world.

Muir's actions helped to save the **Yosemite** Valley and other wilderness areas. He also founded a conservation club, the Sierra Club.

Today you can go to Yosemite National Park and see the park's beauty close up.

Marjory Stoneman Douglas

Hurricane Katrina Volunteers

The Everglades

1947
Douglas writes a book that helps save the Everglades

New Orleans

2005
Volunteers helping survivors of Hurricane Katrina

1945   1965   1985   2005

Douglas fought to save **the Everglades** from draining. Her book *The Everglades: River of Grass*, brought attention to her fight.

Today you can tour the Everglades on Florida's southern tip and see alligators in nature.

Volunteers helped residents as soon as the storm made landfall and continued for more than six months after the storm.

Today New Orleans is still a favorite city among many tourists.

Lesson 1

VOCABULARY

tundra p. 5

megalopolis p. 6

prairie p. 8

Continental Divide p. 10

canyon p. 11

READING SKILL

Compare and Contrast
Copy the chart below.
As you read, use it to
compare and contrast the
Appalachian and Rocky
Mountains.

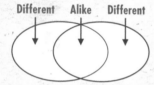

Different   Alike   Different

**New York Academic
Content Standards**
3.1, 3.2

Major LANDFORMS

The Colorado River carved out the Grand Canyon over a period of 6 million years.

Visual Preview

How do landforms affect people and plant life?

A Grasses and mosses grow on the treeless plain near the Arctic Ocean.

B Large cities form a megalopolis along the Atlantic Coastal Plain.

C Farmers grow grains in the fertile soil of the Great Plains.

D Passes allow people to cross the Rocky Mountains.

A THE UNITED STATES AND CANADA

The North American landscape has played a big role in how the United States and Canada grew. It also has amazing physical wonders, such as the Grand Canyon, Rocky Mountains, and the Canadian Shield.

The United States and Canada share most of North America. The western coast faces the Pacific Ocean. The eastern coast faces the Atlantic Ocean. In the north, the very cold Arctic Ocean borders the region. The **tundra**, or a treeless plain, covers Arctic lands in this region where only grasses and mosses can grow. In the south, the Gulf of Mexico's warm currents border the region. Lush grasses grow and thrive in this region.

Canada occupies most of the northern part of North America. It is divided into 13 provinces and territories. Canada is the second–largest country in the world after Russia. The United States is the world's fourth–largest country. Forty-eight of the United States stretch across the middle part of the mainland, or continent, of North America. Two states lie elsewhere. Alaska lies in the northwestern part of the continent. Hawaii is in the Pacific Ocean.

QUICK CHECK

Compare and Contrast **Name two ways in which the United States and Canada are alike.**

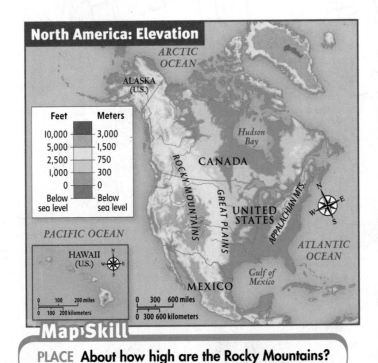

North America: Elevation

ARCTIC OCEAN

ALASKA (U.S.)

Feet	Meters
10,000	3,000
5,000	1,500
2,500	750
1,000	300
0	0
Below sea level	Below sea level

Hudson Bay

ROCKY MOUNTAINS

CANADA

GREAT PLAINS

UNITED STATES

APPALACHIAN MTS.

ATLANTIC OCEAN

PACIFIC OCEAN

HAWAII (U.S.)

Gulf of Mexico

MEXICO

0 100 200 miles
0 100 200 kilometers

0 300 600 miles
0 300 600 kilometers

Map Skill

PLACE **About how high are the Rocky Mountains?**

▲ Because of low temperatures and a short growing season, only grasses and mosses grow in tundra regions.

LOWLANDS AND HIGHLANDS

A variety of landforms shape the United States and Canada. A broad lowland called the Atlantic Coastal Plain runs along the coast of the Atlantic Ocean. The cities of Boston, New York City, Philadelphia, and Washington, D.C., form a **megalopolis** called "Boswash" along the coastal plain. A megalopolis is a group of cities that have grown so close together they seem to form one city. This megalopolis has long been an important economic, cultural, and political center of the United States. Another megalopolis called "ChiPitts" runs from Wisconsin to Toronto, Canada. It includes Milwaukee, Chicago, Detroit, Cleveland, Pittsburgh, and Buffalo.

In northeastern areas of the Atlantic Coastal Plain, the soil is thin and rocky. Farming is limited. However, an area called the Piedmont has fertile soil. The Piedmont lies in the eastern foothills of the Appalachian Mountains alongside the Atlantic Coastal Plain.

Harbors and Ports

Excellent natural harbors along the Atlantic coast have led to the growth of shipping ports. Halifax is a busy port city in the Canadian province of Nova Scotia. About 2,000 ships passed through the port of Halifax in 2007. In that same year the port was responsible for about 9,000 jobs in and around Halifax.

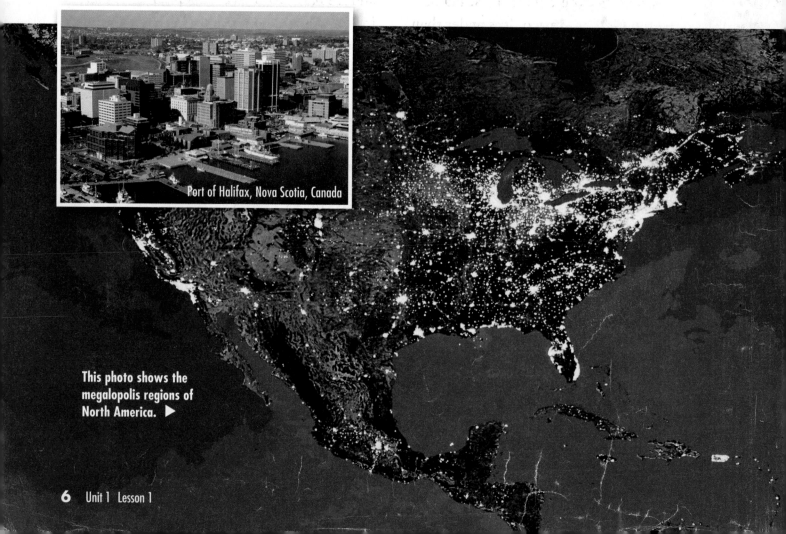

Port of Halifax, Nova Scotia, Canada

This photo shows the megalopolis regions of North America. ▶

Cotton growing on the Gulf Coastal Plain

▲ The view from a hiking trail in the Appalachian Mountains

Another lowland, the Gulf Coastal Plain, lies along the Gulf of Mexico. It is wider than the Atlantic Coastal Plain. Large cities there include Houston and New Orleans. Soil in this region is richer than in the Atlantic Coastal Plain and is excellent for farming. Cotton is a major crop of the Gulf Coastal Plain. Cotton is used to make many things, from books and paper to clothing and dollar bills.

The Appalachian Mountains

West and north of the Atlantic and Gulf Coastal Plains are highland areas. These include the Appalachian Mountains, which run from eastern Canada to Alabama. Geographically, the Appalachians divide the Northeastern states from the Midwestern states. The Appalachian Mountains are the oldest mountains in North America. Their rounded peaks show their age. Water, wind,

and ice have worn away mountain rock and soil in a process called erosion. The highest peak is Mount Mitchell in North Carolina. Even with erosion, it reaches 6,684 feet.

Thousands of people live in the cities and towns of Appalachia. Appalachia is the region in and around the Appalachian Mountains. Many people rely on the natural geography of the area for work. For example, some people have jobs in the coal mining industry. During the 1800s, cities like Charleston, West Virginia, grew rapidly. The city grew because so many people came to work in the coal-rich mines of Appalachia. As the coal mining industry grew, so did other cities and towns.

QUICK CHECK

Compare and Contrast **How are the Atlantic Coastal Plain and the Gulf Coastal Plain different?**

C INTERIOR LOWLANDS

Enormous interior lowlands lie to the west of the eastern highlands. In the north, a horseshoe-shaped area called the Canadian Shield wraps around Hudson Bay. It has rocky hills, lakes, and evergreen forests. With poor soil and a cold climate, the Canadian Shield is not farmable. It does have many minerals, such as iron ore, copper, and nickel. Both mining and logging are thriving industries there.

South of the Canadian Shield and west of the Appalachian Mountains lie the Central Lowlands, or Central Plains. There you will find grassy hills, rolling flatlands, thick forests, and fertile farmland. This area also contains important waterways, such as the Great Lakes and the Mississippi River. Large cities, such as Chicago, Detroit, and Toronto, are located in the Central Plains.

The Great Plains

To the west of the Mississippi River stretch the Great Plains. West of the Mississippi River the land begins to rise. At river's edge, the land is almost at sea level. Over many miles, though, the elevation changes quite a bit. Denver, Colorado, on the western edge of the Great Plains, is about 5,000 feet above sea level!

Much of this vast region is a **prairie**. Prairies are flat, rolling lands covered with grass. The soil is very fertile. Farmers grow grains, and ranchers raise cattle on the land. The Great Plains are also rich in coal, oil, and natural gas.

QUICK CHECK

Compare and Contrast **How are the Canadian Shield and the Great Plains alike?**

Canadian Shield

- ▶ It has rocky hills, lakes, and evergreen forests.
- ▶ Its poor soil and cold climate make it unsuitable for farming.
- ▶ It is rich in minerals such as nickel, copper, and iron ore.

Chart Skill

What kinds of industries would thrive in the Canadian Shield?

The Canadian Shield near Hudson Bay, Canada

Central
Lowlands

The rolling hills of the Midwest

Central Lowlands

▶ You may see rising and falling flatlands, green hills, and dense forests. This region has soil that is good for farming.

▶ There are important waterways such as the Mississippi River and the Great Lakes.

▶ The area is rich in minerals, such as nickel, copper, and iron ore.

▶ Major cities, such as Toronto, Detroit, and Chicago, are located here.

Chart Skill

Why are cities located near waterways?

Great Plains

▶ Much of this vast region has flat, rolling lands covered with grass.

▶ The soil is very fertile.

▶ Farmers grow grains, and ranchers raise cattle.

▶ The region is rich in coal, oil, and natural gas.

Chart Skill

Why do people farm in the Great Plains?

A cattle ranch on the Great Plains

Great Plains

▲ A Great Plains wheat farm

D MOUNTAINS AND PLATEAUS

West of the Great Plains is a group of mountain ranges. The Rocky Mountains begin in Alaska and run south to New Mexico. Although they are younger and higher than the Appalachians, the Rockies have not been a barrier to travel. Mountain passes allow people to cross them.

There is an imaginary line in the Rockies called the **Continental Divide**. East of the Continental Divide, rivers drain into the Arctic Ocean, the Atlantic Ocean, and the Gulf of Mexico. To the west, rivers flow into the Pacific Ocean and the Gulf of California.

LOVELAND PASS
ELEVATION 11,990

CONTINENTAL DIVIDE
ATLANTIC   PACIFIC

▲ Rocky Mountain pass marking the Continental Divide

West   East

River

Diagram Skill

What does the Continental Divide do?

▼ A train traveling through a Rocky Mountain pass

Near the Pacific coast are mountain chains that make up the western part of the group. The highest point in North America, Mount McKinley, rises to 20,320 feet. It is in one of these chains, the Alaska Range. In California the Sierra Nevada range is king. Its tallest point is Mount Whitney at 14,496 feet.

The Grand Canyon

Between these Pacific ranges and the Rocky Mountains is a stretch of dry basins and high plateaus. In the southern part of this area, rivers have worn through rock to create magnificent **canyons**, or deep valleys with steep sides. One of the most beautiful is the Grand Canyon of the Colorado River. A man named John Wesley Powell led the first exploration of the Grand Canyon in 1869.

▲ John Wesley Powell

QUICK CHECK

Compare and Contrast **How are rivers west of the Rocky Mountains different from those in the east?**

▲ President Theodore Roosevelt (left) helped John Muir (right) establish Yosemite National Park in the Sierra Nevada.

Check Understanding

1. **VOCABULARY** Draw a picture to represent one of the words below.

   tundra   prairie   canyon

2. **READING SKILLS** Compare and Contrast Use your chart from page 4 to write a paragraph about the Appalachian and Rocky mountains.

3. **Write About It** Write a paragraph about how the people of Appalachia use their land to live.

Lesson 2

VOCABULARY

navigable p. 13

tributary p. 13

glacier p. 14

wetland p. 16

READING SKILL

Compare and Contrast
As you read, use the chart to compare and contrast the Mississippi and St. Lawrence rivers.

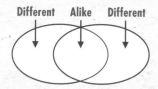

Different   Alike   Different

New York Academic Content Standards
3.1, 3.2

Major Waterways

Bear Mountain Bridge on the Hudson River

Visual Preview

How do people use some of the region's major waterways?

A The Mississippi River is wide and deep enough for large ships to navigate.

B The St. Lawrence Seaway connects the Great Lakes with the Atlantic Ocean.

C People protect the Everglades, home to many rare animals and plants.

A THE MISSISSIPPI RIVER

Native Americans were the first to travel and trade on North American waterways. Over time these same waterways connected major cities and regions of our country.

The United States and Canada have numerous lakes and rivers. Many of the region's rivers are **navigable**, or wide and deep enough to allow the passage of ships.

The second-longest river in the United States is the Mississippi River. The longest is one of its **tributaries**, the Missouri River. A tributary is a river that flows into a larger river. The Mississippi begins as a narrow, unnavigable stream that flows from its source, Lake Itasca in Minnesota, to the Gulf of Mexico.

The Mississippi River Basin dominates the central part of the region. It drains over one million square miles of land. This means that as the river flows from its source to its mouth, the surrounding land is watered and made suitable for farming.

Because so much of the river is wide and deep, ships can navigate the Mississippi for a great distance. Products from port cities such as St. Louis and Memphis are shipped down the river to other ports.

QUICK CHECK

Compare and Contrast **How are navigable and unnavigable rivers similar?**

Mississippi River Basin

Map Skill

REGION **What river regions make up the Mississippi River Basin?**

The mighty Mississippi River

B THE GREAT LAKES

The Great Lakes—the world's largest group of freshwater lakes—lie in the central part of North America. **Glaciers**, or giant blankets of ice, carved Lake Huron, Lake Ontario, Lake Michigan, Lake Erie, and Lake Superior about 10,000 years ago. The largest and deepest of the Great Lakes is Lake Superior. Lake Erie is the most shallow and holds the least water.

St. Lawrence River

The waters of the Great Lakes flow into the St. Lawrence River. The St. Lawrence River flows for about 750 miles from Lake Ontario to the Atlantic Ocean. The Canadian cities of Montreal, Quebec, and Ottawa grew up along the St. Lawrence River and its branches. They depend on the St. Lawrence as an important transportation link.

For many years, rapids, waterfalls, and uneven water levels kept ships from navigating the entire route from the Great Lakes to the Atlantic Ocean. Then, in the mid-1900s, the United States and Canada built a series of canals called the St. Lawrence Seaway. To cope with the problem of changing water levels, engineers built locks. A lock is a part of a canal where water is pumped in or out to raise or lower ships.

Today, ships on the St. Lawrence Seaway carry raw materials and manufactured goods from cities like Chicago, Cleveland, and Toronto to the rest of the world.

QUICK CHECK

Cause and Effect Why did the United States and Canada build the St. Lawrence Seaway?

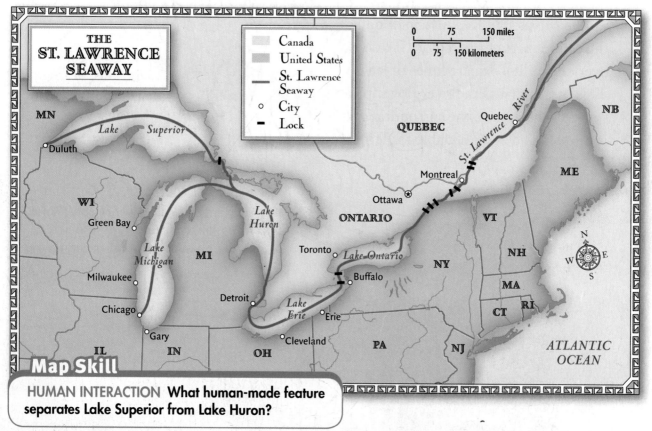

THE ST. LAWRENCE SEAWAY

Canada
United States
— St. Lawrence Seaway
○ City
▬ Lock

0 75 150 miles
0 75 150 kilometers

MN · Duluth · Lake Superior · WI · Green Bay · Lake Michigan · MI · Milwaukee · Chicago · Gary · IL · IN · OH · Detroit · Lake Huron · Lake Erie · Cleveland · Erie · Toronto · Lake Ontario · Buffalo · ONTARIO · Ottawa · Montreal · QUEBEC · Quebec · St. Lawrence River · NB · ME · VT · NH · NY · MA · CT · RI · PA · NJ · ATLANTIC OCEAN

Map Skill

HUMAN INTERACTION What human-made feature separates Lake Superior from Lake Huron?

How a Lock Works

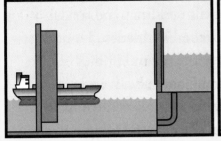

1 Ship enters lock.

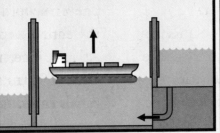

2 Water is pumped in. Ship rises with water level.

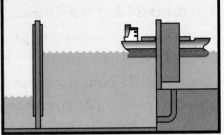

3 Upper lock gates are opened. Ship leaves the lock.

Chart Skill

In what position is the front lock when the rear lock is about to close?

A picture of the Great Lakes from space

C THE EVERGLADES

The Everglades are a large area of **wetlands** in southern Florida. A wetland is an area of land that does not completely drain of water, such as a swamp. Wetlands depend on both water and land to support diverse, sometimes endangered, plant and animal life.

The Everglades are a home for many animals and plants. Alligators, crawfish, falcons, and the rare Florida panther all live in the Everglades.

▲ Alligator

During the late 1800s and early 1900s, people built buildings and roads through the Everglades. To protect and save the natural homes of rare plants and animals, Everglades National Park was created in 1947. Marjory Stoneman Douglas worked tirelessly to preserve the Everglades. Her book, *The Everglades: River of Grass* inspired people to protest the destruction of the Everglades. You can read a section from her book on this page.

Primary Sources

"There are no other Everglades in the world. They are, they have always been, one of the unique regions of the earth; remote, never wholly known. Nothing anywhere else is like them. . . ."

A section from
The Everglades: River of Grass

by Marjory Stoneman Douglas, 1947

Write About It Think about something that should be preserved. Write about ways people can work in your community to promote your cause.

QUICK CHECK

Compare and Contrast **How are lakes and wetlands different?**

Check Understanding

1. **VOCABULARY** Write one sentence for each vocabulary word.

    navigable   glacier   elevation

2. **READING SKILLS** Compare and Contrast Use your chart from page 12 to write a paragraph about the Mississippi and St. Lawrence rivers.

3. **Write About It** How did people change the St. Lawrence Seaway?

Map and Globe Skills
Use Latitude and Longitude Maps

VOCABULARY

global grid
latitude
longitude
absolute location
relative location
parallel
meridian
prime meridian

Some maps divide the Earth into a **global grid**, or set of crisscrossing lines. Lines going from east to west are called **latitude**. Lines going from north to south are called **longitude**. Latitude and longitude are measured in units called degrees. The symbol for degrees is °. The point at which latitude and longitude lines cross is a place's **absolute location**.

Another way to determine the location of a place is by using **relative location**. Relative location tells you where a place or region is located in relation to another place. For example, the relative location of the United States is north of Mexico.

Learn It

- Lines of latitude are called **parallels**. They measure distance north and south of the equator. The equator is labeled 0° latitude. Lines of latitude north of the equator are labeled **N**. Those south of the equator are labeled **S**.

- Lines of longitude are called **meridians**. They measure distance east and west of the **prime meridian** (labeled 0° longitude). Meridians east of the prime meridian are labeled **E**. Meridians west of the prime meridian are labeled **W**.

Latitude and Longitude of the Western Hemisphere

Try It

- Locate Mexico City. Which line of latitude is closest to this city?

- Locate Lima in South America. Which line of longitude is closest to this city?

Apply It

- Find the longitude and latitude lines that are closest to your community.

- Which city is closer to your community in longitude, Mexico City or Lima?

NATURAL RESOURCES

VOCABULARY

renewable resource
p. 20

hydroelectric

power p. 20

scarcity p. 22

economy p. 22

irrigation p. 25

READING SKILL

Compare and Contrast
As you read, use the chart below to compare and contrast energy resources.

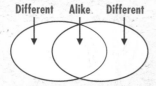
Different   Alike   Different

New York Academic Content Standards
3.1, 3.2, 4.1, 4.2

A forest in Canada

Visual Preview

How do the United States and Canada use natural resources?

A Minerals have helped create industries in the United States and Canada.

B Energy resources include oil, coal, natural gas, wind, sun, and corn.

C The fishing and timber industries have scarce resources.

D Rich soil in parts of Canada and the United States helps farmers grow crops.

Ⓐ MINERAL RESOURCES

Natural resources are materials found in nature that people use. The products and energy we use everyday are made from natural resources. But not all natural resources will last forever.

The United States and Canada have vast mineral resources. A mineral is a natural substance that is found in the earth. Minerals have helped create industries in the United States and Canada.

Parts of eastern Canada and the northern United States have large iron-ore deposits. Iron ore is used to make steel. The Rocky Mountains have gold, silver, and copper. Products made from copper include wire, pipes, and frying pans. Deep within the Canadian Shield are iron ore, copper, nickel, and gold. In fact, the shield supplies Canada with so many different minerals that it is often called "Canada's Storehouse."

QUICK CHECK

Compare and Contrast How are minerals in the Rocky Mountains and the Canadian Shield different?

A gold maple leaf coin ▶

▲ This vibrating table uses water to separate gold ore from rock.

B ENERGY RESOURCES

The United States and Canada have a variety of energy resources. **Renewable resources** are resources that can be replaced. Renewable energy resources include wind, sun, corn, and **hydroelectric power**. Hydroelectric power is energy generated by falling water.

Nonrenewable energy resources include oil, natural gas, and coal. Even with large supplies of oil in Texas and Alaska, the United States imports oil because it uses nearly three times the amount of oil that it produces.

Most of Canada's oil and natural gas reserves lie in or near the province of Alberta. This province has the world's second-largest reserves of oil in the form of oil mixed with sand. A machine called a separator separates the oil from the sand. Canada exports oil and natural gas. Much of these energy exports

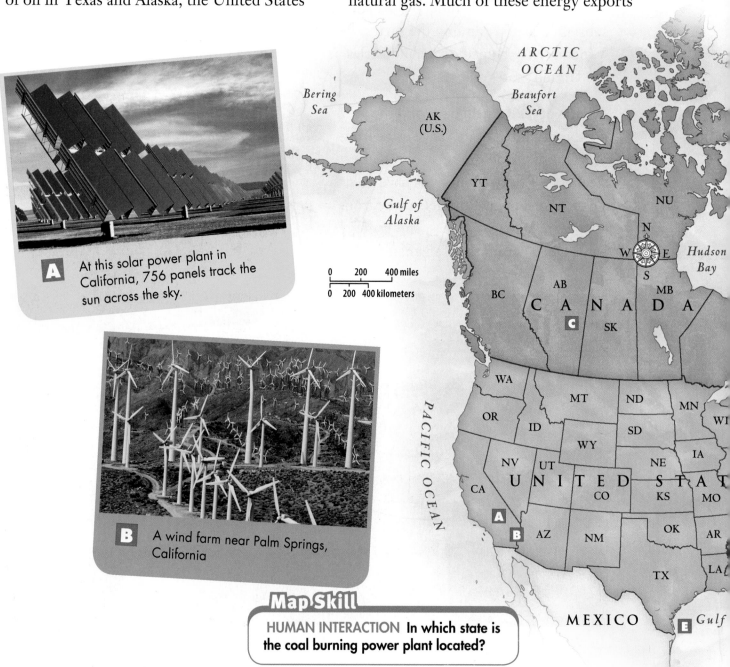

A At this solar power plant in California, 756 panels track the sun across the sky.

B A wind farm near Palm Springs, California

Map Skill

HUMAN INTERACTION **In which state is the coal burning power plant located?**

go to the United States. Coal is mined in many parts of the United States and British Columbia. North America has enough coal to last 400 years, but burning coal pollutes the air and destroys the environment.

Renewable Energy

Scientists have worked to produce renewable sources of energy. Solar energy is made from sunlight. Flat plates called solar panels collect the energy and turn it into electricity. Ethanol is a fuel that is made from corn. Ethanol is used to power cars and rockets. Wind and falling water also make energy. The force of the wind or water spins a turbine that produces electricity. Niagara Falls is a major source of hydroelectric power.

Quick Check

Compare and Contrast How are coal energy and wind energy different?

C An oil separator in Alberta, Canada, separates sand from oil.

D A coal burning power plant in Ohio creates energy from coal.

E Oil rigs in the Gulf of Mexico drill for oil 24 hours a day.

C   SCARCE RESOURCES

Oil and natural gas are limited resources because they are nonrenewable. One day these resources are likely to run out. But even renewable resources can become scarce. Many people are working to improve the **scarcity** of trees and fish. Scarcity happens when there is not enough of a resource to make all of the products people want.

The Timber Industry

Forests once covered much of the United States and Canada. Today, however, forests cover less than 50 percent of Canada and about one-third of the United States. People have cleared land to farm. They also cut forests to make timber products. Farming and timber are important parts of the **economy** of Canada and the United States. A country's economy is the way its people use natural resources, money, and knowledge to produce goods and services.

Loss of Forest in the United States

CANADA

PACIFIC OCEAN

MEXICO

Gulf of Mexico

ATLANTIC OCEAN

☐ Forested areas 8,000 years ago
■ Present-day forested area

0   200   400 miles
0 200 400 kilometers

Map Skill

PLACE **Which state has lost the most forests?**

Lumber and wood products, such as paper, are major exports of Canada. The timber industry is also important to the states of Oregon and Washington.

▼ A logging crew stands with a donkey engine used for hauling logs.

◄ Logging machinery moves logs that were harvested in an old-growth forest in Washington's Cascade Mountains.

An early fishing boat (below) and a current fishing boat (right) in the Atlantic Ocean

GK 101

1354

Catch of Cod in the Northwest Atlantic Ocean, 1950–2002

catch of cod (millions of tons)

year

Chart Skill

In which year was the cod catch largest?

The Fishing Industry

The coastal waters of the Atlantic and Pacific Oceans and the Gulf of Mexico are important to the region's economy. They have fish and shellfish that support fishing industries. In recent years, however, the eastern Atlantic fishing grounds have suffered from overfishing. The Great Banks, located off Canada's southeast coast, were once one of the world's richest fishing grounds. As these waters were overfished, the numbers of fish decreased. The Canadian government banned cod fishing there from 1992 to 1997. At the same time, the freshwater fishing industry has been growing. Lake Winnipeg is the biggest contributor to Canada's freshwater catch.

QUICK CHECK

Compare and Contrast **How are the timber and fishing industries alike?**

Ⓓ SOIL RESOURCES

Rich soil in parts of the United States and Canada help farmers grow crops. Canada's heartland is known as the "Prairie Provinces." It includes Manitoba, Saskatchewan, and Alberta. The map on this page shows you that wheat is the major farm crop in this region.

The area along the St. Lawrence Seaway also has fertile soil. Farmers grow grains, fruits, and vegetables. Dairy farms too are important to the economy of this region.

The Farm Belt

Flat land and fertile soil cover much of the U.S. Midwest. Farmers produce huge amounts of corn, soybeans, and grains such as oats and wheat. In some areas of the Great Plains, farmers use dry farming to grow a certain kind of wheat. Dry farming is a method in which land is left unplanted every few years so it will hold rainwater. Dairy products and livestock are also important to the Midwest economy.

The South's warm, wet climate favors crops that are not usually grown elsewhere in the United States. Farmers in Louisiana and Arkansas, for example, grow rice and sugarcane. In Florida and Texas, they grow citrus fruits such as oranges and lemons. Georgia, Alabama, and North Carolina produce one million tons of peanuts each year.

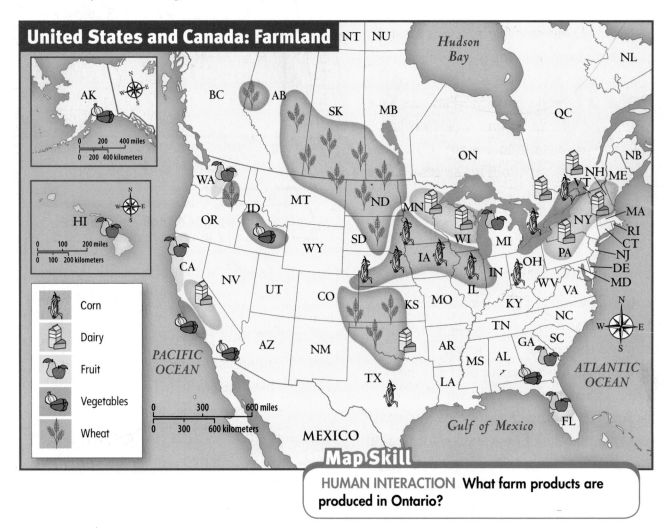

United States and Canada: Farmland

Legend:
- Corn
- Dairy
- Fruit
- Vegetables
- Wheat

Map Skill

HUMAN INTERACTION **What farm products are produced in Ontario?**

A Florida orange grove

Farming Dry Land

The Central Valley of California is located between two mountain ranges, the Sierra Nevada and the Coast Ranges. The land is fertile, and the weather is warm. Farmers have a problem, though. Little rain falls there in the summer because summer is the dry season. For many years farmers could only grow crops that needed little water. They did not have **irrigation**. Irrigation is bringing water to dry land through ditches or pipes.

Today irrigation has made California a leading producer of grapes, olives, plums, peaches, tomatoes, artichokes, and more than 150 other fruits and vegetables. Only Texas grows more cotton than California. Only Florida grows more oranges and grapefruits.

QUICK CHECK

Compare and Contrast **In what ways are California, Texas, and Florida alike?**

Check Understanding

1. **VOCABULARY** Write a paragraph about the fishing industry using these words.

   scarcity   economy

2. **READING SKILLS**
   Compare and Contrast Use your chart from page 18 to write about energy resources.

   Different   Alike   Different

    3. **Write About It** Write about how farmers in California adapted to the dry summer season.

VOCABULARY

temperate climate p. 27

current p. 28

precipitation p. 30

drought p. 30

arid p. 32

READING SKILL

Compare and Contrast
Copy the chart below. As you read, use it to compare and contrast the Northeast and the Pacific Northwest.

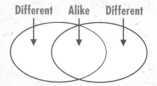

Different   Alike   Different

New York Academic Content Standards
3.1, 3.2

Climate REGIONS

Visual Preview

How does climate affect how people live?

A Long, cold winters and brief, cool summers make life harsh for people.

B People in southern California enjoy warm, dry summers and mild, wet winters.

C People in the deserts see less than 10 inches of rainfall each year.

D In the East, people have plenty of rain.

A   COLD CLIMATES

Climate is the usual pattern of weather in an area over a long period of time. It affects plant life and where people choose to live.

Climate is mainly determined by latitude, but also by landforms such as mountains and large bodies of water. The region of the United States and Canada has a great variety of climates. The far north is a cold, arctic wasteland. Areas near the Tropic of Cancer are warm all year. Most people in the United States and Canada live in a **temperate climate**. Temperate climates have changing seasons and mild weather that is neither too hot nor too cold.

The Far North

The northern arctic parts of Alaska and Canada, winters are long and cold, while summers are brief and cool. As a result, few people live in this harsh environment. The Arctic Ocean's coastline is a treeless tundra. This very cold climate prevents the growth of trees and most plants.

In the subarctic region farther south, dense forests of evergreen trees have adapted to the cold climate. For example, the waxy coating of evergreen needles keeps moisture inside during the bitterly cold winters.

QUICK CHECK

Compare and Contrast **How are the arctic and subarctic regions different?**

▲ Nunavut Native Americans of the Arctic

▼ A Nunavut village

B WARM CLIMATES

Look at the map on page 29. It shows you that warm climates can vary from place to place. In addition to latitude, the movement of air and water helps create Earth's climates. Moving air and water help carry the sun's heat around the globe. In the ocean, the moving streams of water are called **currents**.

The Ocean Effect

Near the Equator, air and water are heated the most. Warm wind and water currents move from the tropics toward the North and South Poles. A large, warm-water ocean current known as the Gulf Stream flows from the Gulf of Mexico through the cool Atlantic Ocean along the east coast of North America.

Water temperatures do not change as much or as fast as land temperatures do. Thus, air over large bodies of water is warmer in winter and cooler in summer. This keeps coastal air temperatures moderate.

The Pacific Coast

The area from southern Alaska to northern California is called the Pacific Northwest. The Pacific Ocean's warm North Pacific Current

Venice Beach in southern California (right) and a Seattle rainstorm (below)

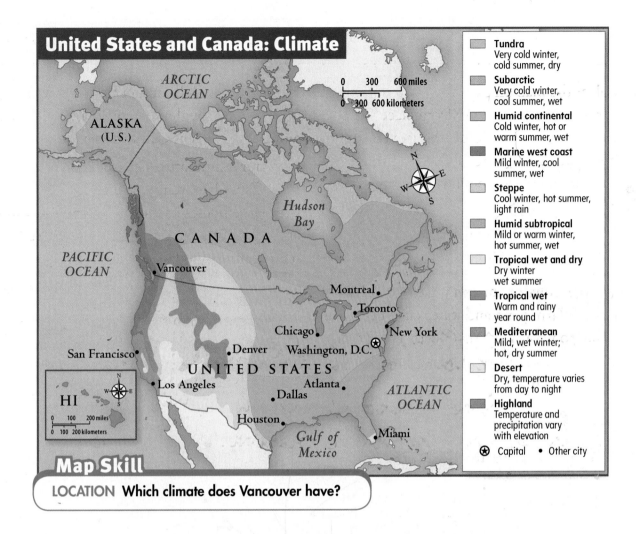

United States and Canada: Climate

Legend:

- **Tundra** Very cold winter, cold summer, dry
- **Subarctic** Very cold winter, cool summer, wet
- **Humid continental** Cold winter, hot or warm summer, wet
- **Marine west coast** Mild winter, cool summer, wet
- **Steppe** Cool winter, hot summer, light rain
- **Humid subtropical** Mild or warm winter, hot summer, wet
- **Tropical wet and dry** Dry winter wet summer
- **Tropical wet** Warm and rainy year round
- **Mediterranean** Mild, wet winter; hot, dry summer
- **Desert** Dry, temperature varies from day to night
- **Highland** Temperature and precipitation vary with elevation
- ⊛ Capital • Other city

Map labels: ARCTIC OCEAN, ALASKA (U.S.), PACIFIC OCEAN, CANADA, Hudson Bay, Vancouver, Montreal, Toronto, Chicago, New York, San Francisco, Denver, Washington, D.C., UNITED STATES, Los Angeles, Atlanta, Dallas, ATLANTIC OCEAN, Houston, Gulf of Mexico, Miami, HI

Scale: 0 300 600 miles / 0 300 600 kilometers

Hawaii inset scale: 0 100 200 miles / 0 100 200 kilometers

Map Skill

LOCATION Which climate does Vancouver have?

keeps this area's climate mild and wet. Evergreen forests, ferns, and mosses are common. By contrast, southern California has a climate of warm, dry summers and mild, wet winters with less rainfall.

Tropical Areas

The tropics lie between the Tropic of Cancer and the Tropic of Capricorn. Temperatures here change little from season to season. Warm tropical climates can be separated into two types. The tropical wet climate is wet in most months, with up to 100 inches of rain a year. The tropical wet and dry climate has a wet season and a dry season.

Two areas of the United States have tropical climates. Southern Florida has a tropical wet and dry climate. Its temperatures are hot in summer and warm in winter. Rain falls mainly in summer.

Hawaii, the other tropical area, has average year-round temperatures in the 70s°F. It has a tropical wet climate. Monthly rainfall, which varies throughout the state, supports tropical rain forests.

QUICK CHECK

Compare and Contrast How are the climates of southern Florida and Hawaii different?

THE DESERT WEST AND MIDWEST

Many parts of the southwestern United States are desert. A desert gets less than 10 inches of precipitation, or rainfall, each year. The Southwest is also closer to the Equator than other parts of the United States. The temperatures are high all year. The heat and dry air affect the region's land.

The Border Deserts

The Sonoran and Chihuahuan deserts cover over 295,000 square miles along the United States-Mexico border. Plants and animals have adapted to this harsh climate over thousands of years. Many plants store water from rainfall so they can survive during the long, dry season.

The Inland West

The inland West stretches from the Sierra Nevada Mountains to the eastern Rocky Mountains. The Great Basin has a steppe climate of hot summers and mild winters. In this region, the Sierra Nevada blocks humid winds from the Pacific Ocean. As a result, the Great Basin receives little rainfall. Plants there survive on little rain.

Areas on the eastern side of the Rockies have a partly dry climate. Drought, or a long period without rainfall, is a serious challenge. Farmers and ranchers can lose crops and animals when rainfall is low.

▼ Acoma Pueblo, New Mexico

▲ A Wyoming rancher leads his horse past a herd of sheep.

The Great Plains

The Great Plains receive their moisture from the Gulf of Mexico and from the Arctic. The eastern part of this area has a humid climate, with cold, snowy winters and hot, humid summers. The western part has light rain. Short grasses and grains grow in this area. Drought sometimes affects the Great Plains. In the 1930s, years of poor farming methods and drought caused the Dust Bowl. The Dust Bowl was a series of windstorms that picked up loose topsoil and turned the central United States and Canada into a wasteland. Economic hardships forced many farmers to leave the Great Plains. Since the 1930s, better farming methods have renewed this area's soil.

The Lake Effect

The Great Lakes affect the land much as the ocean does in other parts of the country. This is called the lake effect. In summer, lake water and the air above it are cooler than the nearby land. Wind crossing a lake creates a cool breeze. In winter the opposite is true. Sometimes, though, winds pick up moisture and form clouds that cause lake effect snow.

EVENT

On April 14, 1935, twenty of the worst Dust Bowl storms turned the day into night. On **Black Sunday** some people could not see five feet in front of them.

Black Sunday

QUICK CHECK

Compare and Contrast **How are the Southwest and inland West alike?**

ⓓ THE EAST

One way to study North America's climate is to divide it into two areas of precipitation, **arid** and humid. Arid regions are dry. In general, the western half of North America is arid. It gets less than 20 inches of precipitation a year. The eastern United States and Canada have humid climate regions. Humid regions receive more than 20 inches of precipitation a year.

The Northeast and Northern Canada

Northeastern areas of the United States have a humid continental climate. They have snowy winters, rainy springs, and hot wet summers. The Northeast gets plenty of precipitation all year.

The forests in the Northeast have two types of trees. One is the broadleaf tree, which has fairly wide leaves. The leaves of this tree change color in autumn.

The other kind of tree is the needleleaf evergreen. These leaves are long and thin, like needles. Needleleaf leaves do not change color in autumn—they stay green all year.

Northern Canada has a subarctic climate. It lies just below the Arctic Circle. The few people living here face severely cold and bitter winters, but temperatures do rise above freezing during summer months. Huge evergreen forests grow in this climate.

▼ Boston park in the summer

Average January and July Temperatures for Boston and Atlanta

	Boston, MA	Atlanta, GA
Average January Temperature	28.6°F (−1.9°C)	41.0°F (5.0°C)
Average July Temperature	73.5°F (23.0°C)	78.8°F (26.0°C)

Chart Skill
Which city is warmer in July?

▲ Atlanta's Centennial Olympic Park

▼ Boston's Common (public) Gardens during a snowstorm

The Southeast

The Southeast has a humid subtropical climate. Rain falls throughout the year but is less heavy during the hot and humid summer months. Humid subtropical winters are generally short and mild.

Although many crops can be grown in cooler climates, the warm Southeast region is the only place where certain crops, such as cotton, can be grown. This is because the Southeast has a longer growing season than some other regions of the United States. A growing season is the number of days in a year when crops can grow.

QUICK CHECK

Compare and Contrast **How are the Northeast United States and Northern Canada climates different?**

Check Understanding

1. **VOCABULARY** Write about the Great Basin using the following words.

   precipitation   drought   arid

2. **READING SKILLS** Compare and Contrast Use your chart from page 26 to write about the Northeast and the Pacific Northwest.

3. **Write About It** Write a paragraph about ways people need to adapt to their desert environments.

Lesson 5

READING SKILL

Compare and Contrast
Copy the chart below. As you read, use it to compare and contrast earthquakes and volcanic eruptions.

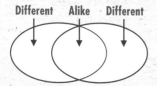

Different   Alike   Different

New York Academic Content Standards
1.4, 3.1, 3.2

Environmental CHALLENGES

Mount Saint Helens erupting in 1982

Visual Preview

How do natural disasters affect people?

A Tornadoes can level houses, knock down trees, and toss cars.

B Extreme weather can cause power failures, flooding, and can damage buildings.

C Earthquakes and volcanoes can destroy entire cities.

D Global warming may bring higher temperatures and rising water levels.

A   TORNADOES

People adapt to their climate to survive. But in certain areas of North America natural disasters bring vast destruction. Most natural disasters cannot be prevented. In some cases, however, people do play a role.

Some areas of the United States and Canada are more likely to experience severe weather than others. Severe weather includes wind, rain, and lightning. It can destroy buildings and result in massive flooding.

"Tornado Alley"

Look at the map on this page. As you can see, a large part of the Midwest is more likely to experience a tornado than are other parts of the country. A **tornado** is a powerful windstorm with a funnel-shaped cloud that moves quickly over land. The high winds of a tornado can level houses, knock down trees, and toss cars around. The central United States sees more tornadoes each year than any other place in the world. In fact, tornados are so common from Texas north to Nebraska that this area has been nicknamed "Tornado Alley."

EVENT

The deadliest tornado in U.S. history was the **Great Tri-State Tornado** of 1925. It crossed through Missouri, Illinois, and Indiana, killing 695 people. The tornado killed twice as many people as the second deadliest tornado in 1840.

Great Tri-State Tornado

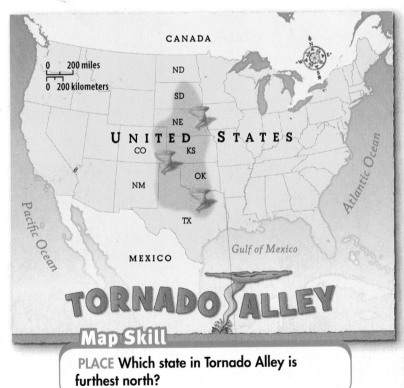

TORNADO ALLEY

Map Skill

PLACE **Which state in Tornado Alley is furthest north?**

QUICK CHECK

Compare and Contrast **In what way are Texas and Nebraska alike?**

HURRICANES AND BLIZZARDS

B

Like tornadoes, **hurricanes** are funnel-shaped wind systems. But hurricanes are much larger. They develop over large bodies of warm water and lose their strength over land. Coastal regions can receive a lot of damage from a hurricane, while inland areas are relatively safe.

Storm Surge

Hurricanes combine with normal tides to create a storm tide. Wind pushes the storm tide to shore creating the storm surge. These high waters can flood low-lying coastal areas. Hurricanes generally develop from June to September. They most often strike along the southeastern Atlantic coast and the Gulf of Mexico. In other parts of the world hurricanes are called cyclones or typhoons. Cyclone describes the storm's cyclonic nature, which means that its circulation is counterclockwise in the Northern Hemisphere and clockwise in the Southern Hemisphere.

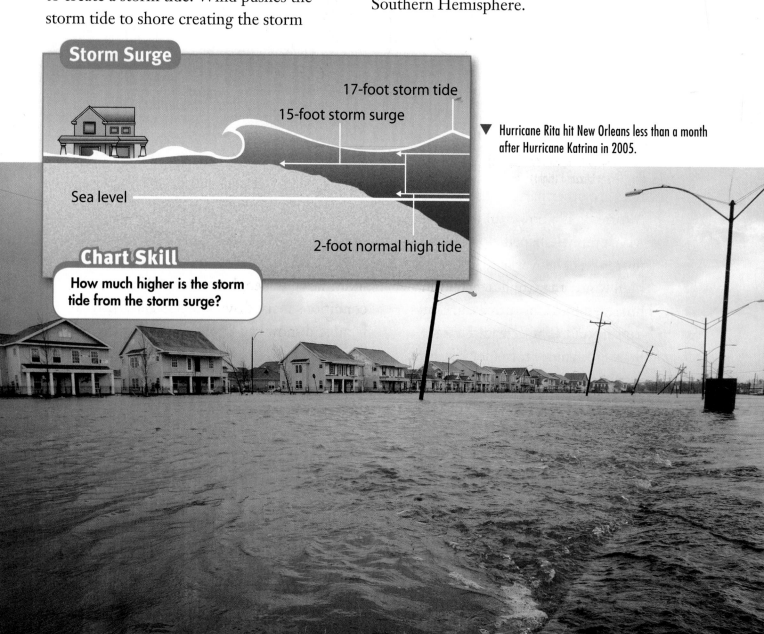

Storm Surge

17-foot storm tide

15-foot storm surge

Sea level

2-foot normal high tide

Chart Skill

How much higher is the storm tide from the storm surge?

▼ Hurricane Rita hit New Orleans less than a month after Hurricane Katrina in 2005.

▲ A blizzard in New York City in 1888 (above) and a more recent blizzard (right) ▶

One of the most damaging hurricanes in history, Hurricane Katrina, struck the Gulf coast in August of 2005. It damaged a wide area from Mobile, Alabama, to New Orleans, Louisiana.

More than 1,800 people died, and hundreds of thousands lost their homes. Most of New Orleans and many nearby towns were completely flooded. In Mississippi, entire towns were leveled.

Blizzards

Blizzards bring their own hazards. Blizzards are severe winter storms that last several hours and combine high winds with heavy snow that limits how far people can see. "White-out" conditions make driving dangerous. Also, the wind and snow can knock down electric power lines and trees. Blizzards can bring human activity in a busy city to a halt for days as cities work to clear the streets. In the United States, blizzards are common in the Northeast. The Great Blizzard of 1888 shut down New York City. It killed 400 people and sank 200 ships. Snow drifts towered 15 to 50 feet high.

QUICK CHECK

Compare and Contrast How are hurricanes and blizzards alike?

EARTHQUAKES AND VOLCANOES

Scientists have developed a theory about the earth's structure called **plate tectonics**. This theory states that the surface of Earth is made up of moving plates, or huge slabs of rock. These plates fit together like a jigsaw puzzle. They move—sometimes slowly, sometimes suddenly—atop soft rock. Oceans and continents ride on top of the gigantic plates.

Moving Plates

The plates can push against each other or pull apart from each other. These movements take place along faults, or cracks, that separate the plates. Shifts along a fault can cause earthquakes, or violent jolts, in the area around it. In coastal areas, earthquakes can cause huge waves, known as tsunamis. In 2004 a tsunami in the Indian Ocean killed about 230,000 people along coastal areas.

In North America, many earthquakes occur along the Pacific coast. This region lies along a major fault zone. A 1906 earthquake damaged most of the buildings in San Francisco. Many buildings were destroyed by fires triggered by broken natural gas mains. Because of the danger of powerful earthquakes, buildings in these areas now are built in special ways to protect them from damage.

Volcanoes

The area where two plates meet can also be the site of volcanoes. A volcano forms

Trees floating in a lake (below) and a damaged car (right) after the 1980 Mount Saint Helens eruption

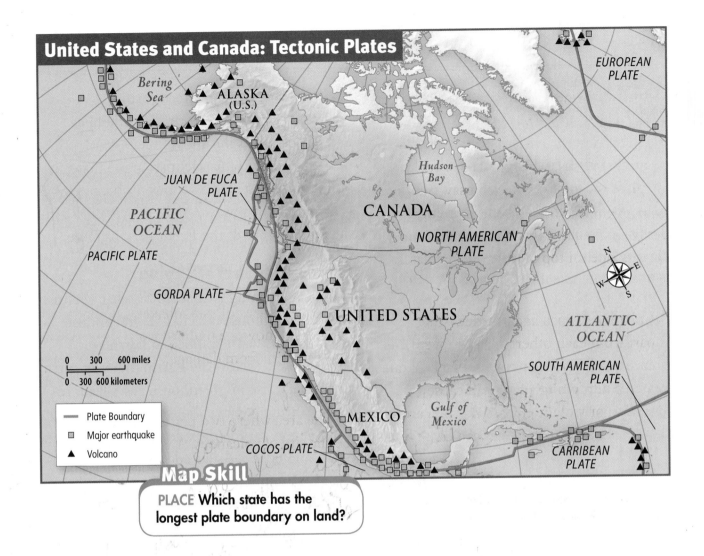

United States and Canada: Tectonic Plates

EUROPEAN PLATE

Bering Sea

ALASKA (U.S.)

JUAN DE FUCA PLATE

PACIFIC OCEAN

PACIFIC PLATE

GORDA PLATE

Hudson Bay

CANADA

NORTH AMERICAN PLATE

UNITED STATES

ATLANTIC OCEAN

SOUTH AMERICAN PLATE

0   300   600 miles
0   300   600 kilometers

Gulf of Mexico

MEXICO

COCOS PLATE

CARRIBEAN PLATE

Plate Boundary
☐ Major earthquake
▲ Volcano

Map Skill

PLACE **Which state has the longest plate boundary on land?**

when magma, or molten rock, breaks through Earth's crust as lava. How does this shape the land? Volcanoes may explode in a fiery burst of ashes and rock. Then a cone-shaped mountain such as Washington's Mount Saint Helens, results. Sometimes lava flows slowly, building up rounded mountains such as those in Hawaii.

Volcanoes are found in the Pacific Coast mountains, southern Alaska, and Hawaii. Most are now dormant, or not ready to erupt soon. A few of Hawaii's volcanoes are still active.

Yellowstone Caldera in Yellowstone National Park was a supervolcano. Supervolcanoes are large volcanoes that usually have a large crater and can potentially produce

devastation on an enormous scale. Such eruptions would cause severe cooling of global temperatures for many years afterward. This would happen because of the huge volumes of ash that would erupt.

Hawaii is an example of a place where volcanoes erupt with huge quantities of lava that gradually build wide mountains with shield-like profiles. The largest lava shield on Earth is Mauna Loa, which forms part of the island of Hawaii.

QUICK CHECK

Compare and Contrast **How are earthquakes and volcanic eruptions alike?**

DataGraphic

Global Warming

The map shows how much Arctic ice has retreated, or melted. The graph predicts the rise in sea levels. Study the map and graph. Then answer the questions below.

Arctic Sea Ice Levels

RUSSIA

0   400 miles
0   400 kilometers

ARCTIC OCEAN   +North Pole

Beaufort Sea

ALASKA (U.S.)

GREENLAND

☐ September 2006
--- Historical average

CANADA

Predicted Global Sea Level Rise

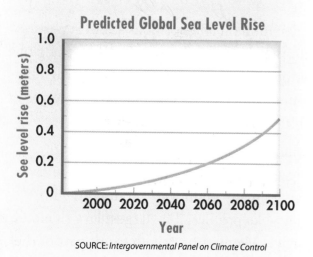

See level rise (meters)

1.0
0.8
0.6
0.4
0.2
0

2000 2020 2040 2060 2080 2100

Year

SOURCE: *Intergovernmental Panel on Climate Control*

Think About Global Warming

1. About how much has Arctic ice melted?
2. How much might sea levels rise by 2040?

Human activity can affect Earth's environment. Most factories, automobiles, and power plants burn fossil fuels—coal, oil, or natural gas. Many scientists argue that this pollution has created a serious problem: **global warming**. Global warming is an overall rise in the temperature of the Earth's atmosphere.

Causes of Global Warming

Global warming is affected by what scientists call the greenhouse effect. The greenhouse effect is heat that is trapped in Earth's atmosphere to warm the Earth. Many scientists claim that a rise in greenhouse gases leads to global warming. Greenhouse gases include water vapor, carbon dioxide, methane, nitrous oxide, and ozone. As we add greenhouse gases to the air, temperatures rise. Ice caps at the poles begin to melt, and ocean waters rise.

Some scientists believe that the rise in temperatures from global warming can also cause extreme weather conditions, including powerful hurricanes. An increase in global temperatures can cause rising sea levels and changes in the amount and pattern of precipitation. These changes may cause floods, droughts, heat waves, and tornadoes.

PEOPLE

Through books and television, **David Suzuki** has educated people about the threat of global warming. In 2004, television viewers voted Suzuki the greatest living Canadian.

David Suzuki

▲ This glacier on Mount Baker, Washington has been rapidly melting since 1980.

The Future

Some scientists say that to solve the problem of global warming we need to change the way we produce energy. One way would be to use more clean and renewable sources of energy. These include sun, wind, and fuels such as ethanol, which is made from corn. Countries such as Denmark produce large amounts of energy with huge windmills. Someday, we may even place huge panels in space to collect solar energy and send it back to Earth.

QUICK CHECK

Compare and Contrast **In what ways can energy sources be different?**

Check Understanding

1. **VOCABULARY** Draw a picture to represent one of the words below.

   tornado   hurricane   blizzard

2. **READING SKILLS**
   Compare and Contrast Use your chart from page 34 to write about earthquakes and volcanoes.

   Different   Alike   Different

 3. **Write About It** Write about the human activities that can cause global warming.

Lesson 6

VOCABULARY

levee p. 44

water table p. 45

READING SKILL

Compare and Contrast
Copy the chart below. As you read, use it to compare and contrast New Orleans before 1900 and after.

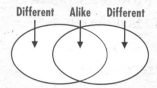

Different   Alike   Different

New York Academic Content Standards
1.4, 3.1, 3.2

Hurricane Katrina and New Orleans

Hurricane Katrina pounding the Gulf Coast

Visual Preview

Why was New Orleans heavily damaged by a hurricane?

A Hurricane Katrina was one of the worst natural disasters in history.

B Most of New Orleans is below sea level, with levees holding back water.

Ⓐ THE STORM

Hurricane Katrina was the costliest and one of the deadliest hurricanes in the history of the United States. Hundreds of thousands of people lost their homes and livelihoods. Katrina also forced thousands of people to move to other parts of the United States.

On August 29, 2005, Hurricane Katrina struck the Gulf coast of the United States. The hurricane blasted the region with winds of more than 140 miles per hour. It caused a storm surge of more than 30 feet and brought as many as 16 inches of rainfall in a matter of hours.

The Damage

The wind, waves, and rain caused flooding that stretched from Louisiana to Mississippi and Alabama. More than 1,800 people died, and property damage was more than $81 billion. It was one of the worst natural disasters in American history.

Many towns and cities suffered greatly from Katrina, but New Orleans probably suffered the most. Most of its almost 450,000 people had fled the city before the storm arrived. That decision proved wise. The city was almost completely flooded when flood barriers broke a few days after the storm. The people that remained in the city took cover in a football stadium. Damage was so severe that even a year later, fewer than half of the city's people had returned.

QUICK CHECK

Compare and Contrast **In what way are Hurricane Katrina and the 2004 tsunami alike?**

Flood-ravaged St. Bernard Parish, Louisiana, after Hurricane Katrina

Both the location of New Orleans and the shape of its land played roles in the Katrina disaster. New Orleans is almost surrounded by water. Lake Pontchartrain lies north of the city. The Mississippi River flows to the west and south. The city of New Orleans has the lowest elevation in the state of Louisiana. It is the third lowest point in the United States, after Death Valley and the Salton Sea. Much of the city is one to ten feet below sea level.

Citizenship

Express Your Opinion

How can expressing your opinion bring change? After Hurricane Katrina, many people expressed their opinion about the slow response of the Federal Emergency Management Agency (FEMA). Their outrage led to a U.S. Congressional investigation. Voting is one way to express your opinion. Another way is by writing to your mayor, governor, or member of Congress about issues you care about. You can also write an editorial for your local newspaper or Web site. Expressing an opinion is a right all American citizens enjoy.

Write About It Write an editorial that expresses your opinion about an issue in your community.

A Bowl-shaped City

In addition, New Orleans is built on a bit of land that is like the bottom of a bowl, with the lake and river forming the rim of the bowl. Under the right conditions high waters could spill over the banks of the lake and the river to flood the city.

The people of New Orleans had long been aware of this danger. To prevent flooding, they built a complex system of **levees**, high walls along the banks of the river and lake.

During and after the storms, winds and rushing storm waters caused several levees to burst open. When that happened, water from the lake and river poured into the city and covered much of it in a deep flood.

Hurricane Damage Factors

Hurricane damage is caused by three factors: storm surge, wind, and flooding. Approximately 90 percent of all hurricane deaths can be blamed on the storm surge. Wind can cause widespread destruction far inland of coastal areas. Finally, hurricanes dump many inches of rain over a widespread area in a short period of time. This water can overflow rivers and streams, causing massive flooding.

The Older Neighborhoods

About 20 percent of New Orleans did not flood in the days following Hurricane Katrina. Areas above sea level are primarily those next to the Mississippi River. These were the areas built between 1719 and 1900. They include the famous French Quarter.

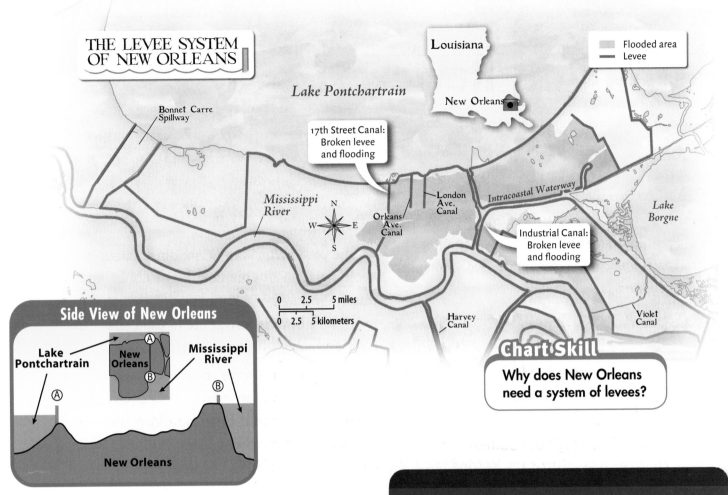

THE LEVEE SYSTEM OF NEW ORLEANS

Lake Pontchartrain

Louisiana

New Orleans

Flooded area
Levee

Bonnet Carre Spillway

17th Street Canal: Broken levee and flooding

Mississippi River

London Ave. Canal

Intracoastal Waterway

Lake Borgne

Orleans Ave. Canal

Industrial Canal: Broken levee and flooding

N
W E
S

0   2.5   5 miles
0   2.5   5 kilometers

Harvey Canal

Violet Canal

Side View of New Orleans

Lake Pontchartrain

New Orleans

Mississippi River

Ⓐ

Ⓑ

New Orleans

Chart Skill

Why does New Orleans need a system of levees?

The rainwater in New Orleans is pumped into Lake Pontchartrain through a series of canals lined by levees. Because of the city's high **water table**, or underground water that is close to the surface, most houses do not have basements. In cemeteries, most tombs are aboveground. In 1995 a heavy rain exposed the weaknesses of the pumping system and flooded the city. The city has considered passing a law that would require all new homes to have a garage and storage level on the first floor to protect people's living spaces from floodwaters.

QUICK CHECK

Compare and Contrast **In what way are hurricanes and earthquakes alike?**

Check Understanding

1. **VOCABULARY** Draw a diagram of one of the vocabulary terms below.

   levee   water table

2. **READING SKILLS** Compare and Contrast Use your chart from page 42 to write about New Orleans.

   Different Alike Different

3. **Write About It** Write about why people would build a city below sea level.

Unit 1 Review

Vocabulary

Number a paper from 1 to 4. Beside each number write the word from the list below that matches the description.

tundra   drought

glacier   levee

1. a long period without rain
2. a treeless plain where only grasses and mosses can grow
3. a high wall built to protect areas from flooding
4. a giant blanket of ice

Comprehension and Critical Thinking

5. Why is the Canadian Shield valuable despite its cold climate and rugged landscape?
6. What are some of the causes of global warming?
7. **Reading Skill** How are tornadoes and hurricanes alike?
8. **Critical Thinking** How can mountains in a region affect climate?

Skill

Use Latitude and Longitude Maps

Write a complete sentence to answer each question.

9. Toronto is about how many degrees north of Washington, D.C.?
10. What is the absolute location of Vancouver?

Latitude and Longitude

New York Social Studies Test Preparation

Base your answers to questions 1 through 3 on the map below and on your knowledge of social studies.

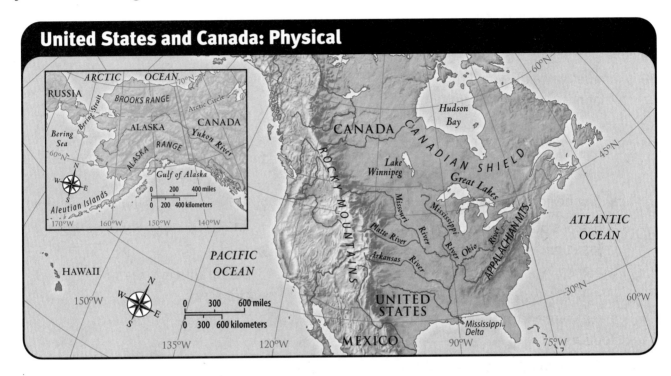

United States and Canada: Physical

1 The information on the map is mostly about

(A) elevation

(B) population

(C) landforms and latitude

(D) products and resources

2 In which direction would a person travel if he or she took a train directly from the Appalachian Mountains to Lake Winnipeg?

(A) northeast

(B) northwest

(C) southeast

(D) southwest

3 Which latitude is closest to the Mississippi delta?

(A) 30° S

(B) 30° N

(C) 90° W

(D) 90° E

How do people adapt to where they live?

Write About the Big Idea

Expository Essay

Use the Unit 1 Foldable to help you write an expository essay that answers the Big Idea question, *How do people adapt to where they live?* Be sure to begin your essay with an introduction. Use the notes you wrote under the tabs in the Foldable for details to support each main idea. Be sure to include ways that people change their environment and ways that people are affected by it.

FOLDABLES™
Study Organizer

Ways people change their environment

Ways people are affected by their environment

Create a Newspaper Article

Work in small groups to create a front page news story about an event that you have read about in Unit 1. There are several parts to an article.

1. One person should write the article.

2. One person should find and cut out or copy photographs and illustrations for the page.

3. Another person should find and make a copy of a map or chart that helps to explain the story.

Decide as a group how you want your page to look. Then decide as a group what the headline will be.

GLOBAL WARMING
Polar Bears' Habitat Melting

Global warming is a threat to the survival of polar bears. The World Conservation Union has estimated that the polar bear population will drop by 30 percent over the next 45 years. In Canada, numbers fell by 22 percent between 1997 and 2004.

Unit 2

EXPLORE The Big Idea

Essential Question
How do people affect the history and culture of a region?

FOLDABLES™ Study Organizer

Cause and Effect
Make and label a three-tab Foldable book before you read this unit. Across the top write: **How people affect a region**. Label the three tabs: **History**, **Government**, and **Culture**. Use the Foldable to organize information as you read.

How people affect a region

History	Government	Culture

LOG ON For more about Unit 2, go to www.macmillanmh.com

The flags of Canada and the United States frame this across-the-border picnic in the village of Coutts, Alberta, Canada.

United States and Canada:
From Past to Present

PEOPLE, PLACES, AND EVENTS

James Wolfe

Plains of Abraham, Quebec

1759
British defeat the French in Canada during the Seven Years' War

Martha Washington

Valley Forge, Pennsylvania

1778
Martha Washington helps troops during the winter at Valley Forge

1750   1760   1770   1850

General James Wolfe and his men scrambled to the **Plains of Abraham** to defeat the French and take Quebec.

Today you can see the park where the battle took place and even enjoy an outdoor concert.

Martha Washington nursed General George Washington's troops during the harsh winter at **Valley Forge, Pennsylvania**.

Today Valley Forge Historical Park recreates how soldiers survived harsh conditions.

Abraham Lincoln

Fort Sumter, South Carolinia

1861
The Civil War begins with the first battle at Fort Sumter

Martin Luther King, Jr.

Washington, D. C.

1963
Citizens march on Washington demanding civil rights

1860   1870   1960   1970

After **Abraham Lincoln** was elected President, the South went to war. The first battle took place at **Fort Sumter**, **South Carolina**.

Today you can take a 30-minute boat ride from Charleston to visit Fort Sumter National Park.

Civil-rights leader **Martin Luther King**, **Jr.**, gave a speech about civil rights at the march.

Today you can visit the Lincoln Memorial in **Washington**, **D. C.**, where King delivered his famous speech.

Lesson 1

VOCABULARY

indigenous p. 53

treaty p. 56

annex p. 56

slavery p. 56

terrorism p. 59

READING SKILL

Cause and Effect

Copy the chart below. As you read, fill it in with the causes and effects of wars Americans have fought.

Cause	→	Effect
	→	
	→	
	→	

New York Academic Content Standards

1.1, 1.2, 1.3, 1.4

History of the United States

The Statue of Liberty is a symbol of freedom for all Americans.

Visual Preview

How do people contribute to the history of the United States?

A The Iroquois wrote laws that influenced the United States Constitution.

B George Washington led the Revolution and was the first President.

C The Lewis and Clark expedition explored western lands of the United States.

D Rosa Parks was a leader in the civil rights movement.

A THE FIRST AMERICANS

For thousands of years, people of different ways of life have been living in what is now the United States. Over the years, Americans have fought in wars at home and abroad. Many also had to fight for their civil rights.

About 10,000 to 15,000 years ago, the first Americans settled the Americas. They were hunters from Asia who probably followed herds of animals across a land bridge to Alaska. Many also may have come to the Americas by boat. People who are descendants of the first groups are call **indigenous** people. In the United States, indigenous people are called Native Americans.

▲ The Iroquois wrote laws that influenced the United States Constitution.

Ways of Life

Over many centuries, Native Americans developed different ways of life using local resources. Some grew corn in the desert. Others hunted deer in the forests and cut down trees to build homes and canoes. In the Plains, buffalo provided people with food, clothing, and shelter. Other Native Americans caught salmon and other fish in the Pacific Ocean.

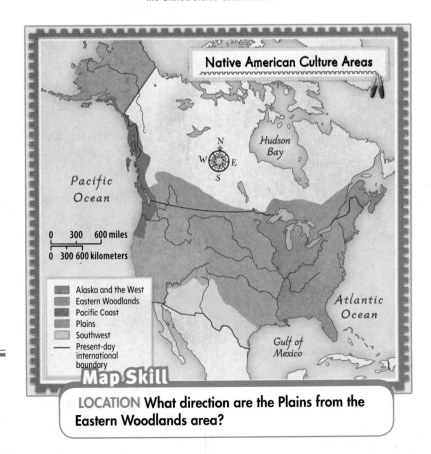

Native American Culture Areas

Pacific Ocean

Hudson Bay

0 300 600 miles
0 300 600 kilometers

- Alaska and the West
- Eastern Woodlands
- Pacific Coast
- Plains
- Southwest
- — Present-day international boundary

Atlantic Ocean

Gulf of Mexico

Map Skill

LOCATION **What direction are the Plains from the Eastern Woodlands area?**

QUICK CHECK

Cause and Effect **Why did Native Americans develop different ways of living?**

B THE COLONIAL ERA

The Pilgrims arrived in Massachusetts in 1620.

Native American ways of life changed after 1492. In that year, explorer Christopher Columbus, sailing west from Europe, reached islands in the Caribbean Sea.

European Settlements

European countries soon set up colonies. Colonies are settlements far away from the country that rules them. Native Americans fought for their land. Some died in wars, but most died from the diseases that Europeans brought to the Americas.

European Colonies in North America, 1763

- British land
- French land
- Spanish land
- Disputed or lands unclaimed by Europeans
- Proclamation Line of 1763

Map Skill

MOVEMENT Which part of North America did France control after 1763?

France, Great Britain, and Spain set up colonies in North America. Great Britain settled in Virginia in 1607. Eventually it had 13 colonies along the Atlantic coast. In 1763 the British defeated France in a war and won control of its colonies.

PEOPLE

Metacomet, or King Phillip, as the British called him, was a Wampanoag Indian. He led his people in a war against the English colonists.

Metacomet

The American Revolution

The people in Great Britain's 13 colonies soon grew angry over British taxes and trade policies. In 1776 the colonists declared their independence. But Great Britain would not give up its colonies without a fight.

The Revolutionary War lasted eight years. General George Washington was commander of the Continental army. One of the darkest times of the war was the winter camp at Valley Forge near Philadelphia. There, supplies were low and 2,500 men died of disease. Martha Washington, the wife of George Washington, helped nurse and comfort the sick. But the Patriots did not give up. They fought on and won several battles. Finally, in 1783 Britain recognized American independence. A new nation called the United States was born.

QUICK CHECK

Cause and Effect **What effect did British taxes and trade policies have on the colonists?**

George Washington became the first President of the United States. ▶

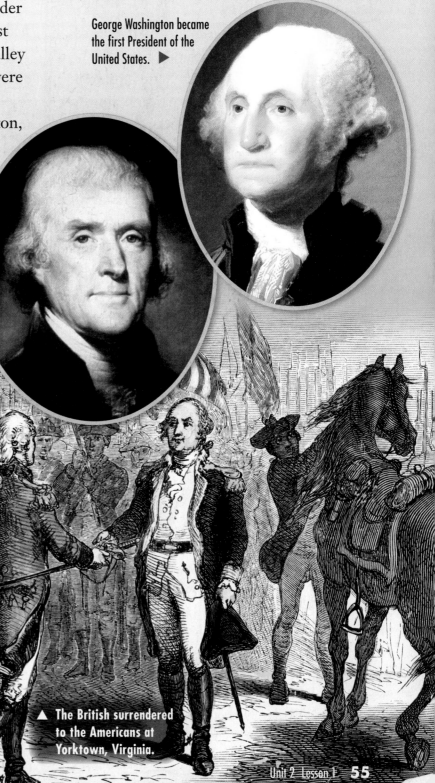

Thomas Jefferson was the author of the Declaration of Independence. ▶

▲ The British surrendered to the Americans at Yorktown, Virginia.

C EXPANSION AND DIVISION

By 1783 the United States had gained land west of the Appalachian Mountains. During the 1800s, the United States expanded all the way to the Pacific Ocean.

A Growing Country

Some of this growth came through **treaties**, or written agreements, with other nations. Some came when the United States **annexed**, or took over, an area. This expansion, however, brought suffering to Native Americans who had lived on their land for centuries. They lost their land, their culture, and often their lives.

Throughout the 1800s, the United States grew in population as well. High birth rates, better public health, and the arrival of millions of Europeans increased the population.

The American economy also grew. New machines made it faster and easier for farmers to plant and harvest crops. Manufacturers developed the factory system to produce many goods faster. Roads, canals, steamboats, and railroads were able to move goods more quickly to markets.

A Divided Country

By the 1850s, social and economic differences divided the country into two regions—North and South. Industry and trade were important in the northern states. The southern states built their economy on agriculture and **slavery**. Slavery is the practice of owning people and forcing them to work.

During this time, people in the North increasingly criticized slavery. Some worked on a system of secret land routes to help people escaping slavery reach the North. This system was called the Underground Railroad. Harriet Tubman, an escaped slave, rescued hundreds on the railroad. Southerners worried that Northerners would move to end slavery.

▼ Sacajawea guided Lewis and Clark as they explored the Louisiana Territory.

United States, 1783

NH
MA
NY
RI
CT
PA
NJ
DE
MD
ATLANTIC OCEAN
Ohio River
Mississippi River
VA
NC
SC
GA
disputed area
Gulf of Mexico

0   200   400 miles
0   200   400 kilometers

British North America
United States of America
Spanish colony
1783 boundary

Map Skill

MOVEMENT **By about how much did the United States grow from 1776 to 1783?**

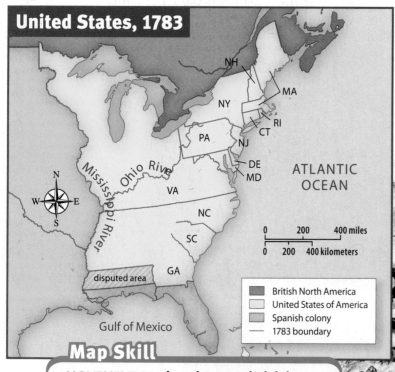

▲ Harriet Beecher Stowe's novel *Uncle Tom's Cabin* described to many Northerners the evils of slavery.

Enslaved Africans working on a sugar plantation in the South

The Civil War

Abraham Lincoln did not want slavery to spread to other states. When he was elected President in 1860, the South set up its own country. The divided nation went to war.

For many, the Civil War was about keeping the Union together. That changed in January 1863, when President Lincoln issued the Emancipation Proclamation. It freed all enslaved Africans in the rebellious states. The Civil War was now a war to end slavery.

At the end of 1863, Lincoln delivered his Gettysburg Address, reminding Americans that the United States was based on the belief that "all men are created equal."

The fighting ended in 1865. The North had won. Slavery was ended. But the newly freed African Americans still faced poverty and discrimination in the years ahead.

QUICK CHECK

Cause and Effect **What effect did United States expansion have on Native Americans?**

Primary Sources

❝I had reasoned this out in my mind, there was one of two things I had a right to, liberty or death; if I could not have one, I would have the other.❞

Harriet Tubman, as told to Sarah Bradford, *Harriet, the Moses of Her People*, 1869.

Write About It Suppose you worked to help people escape slavery. Write a journal entry describing a day of work.

We Can Do It!

▲ "Rosie the Riveter" (left) encouraged women to work for the war effort. Women built war planes (center and right) during World War II.

Ⓓ A WORLD LEADER

In the late 1800s, industry spread in the United States. Waves of new immigrants provided workers for the growing economy. By 1900, the United States was one of the world's major industrial countries.

World Wars

During the 1900s, the United States became a world leader. It took part in World War I and World War II. During these conflicts, United States leaders pushed for the world's people to fight for freedom against cruel and unfair governments. American factories made tanks and airplanes. American soldiers fought in the battlefields. In 1945 the United States and its allies, Great Britain, France and the Soviet Union won World War II.

The Cold War

After World War II, the United States and the Soviet Union became the world's two major powers. The Soviet Union sent troops into Eastern Europe and put these countries under Soviet rule. The Soviets did not allow the countries to hold free elections. These actions led to the Cold War. The Cold War was a war fought with ideas, words, money, and sometimes force.

Both countries began a race to build atomic and other deadly weapons. People in both countries were afraid the other country would attack. In 1989 anti-Soviet protests began the break up of the Soviet Union. Two years later the Cold War ended.

Equal Rights

During the mid-1900s, African Americans, migrant farm workers, Native Americans, women, and people with disabilities became more active in seeking equal rights.

In 1955 Rosa Parks sparked the fight for equal rights when she refused to move from the whites-only section of a Montgomery, Alabama, bus. In 1963 Martin Luther King, Jr., led a march to Washington. In a famous speech, he said,

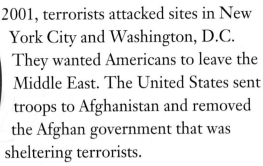

Rosa Parks

❝I have a dream that one day this nation will rise up and live out the true meaning of its creed: 'We hold these truths to be self-evident, that all men are created equal.'❞

21st Century Challenges

Since 2000, the United States has faced challenges from the growth of **terrorism**. Terrorism is the use of violence or threats to reach a political goal. On September 11, 2001, terrorists attacked sites in New York City and Washington, D.C. They wanted Americans to leave the Middle East. The United States sent troops to Afghanistan and removed the Afghan government that was sheltering terrorists.

In 2003 U.S. troops overthrew Iraq's government. Many people believed Iraq had weapons of mass destruction that it could use against its neighbors. In the years that followed, the United States worked with Afghanistan and Iraq to set up new governments. Continued fighting within both countries, however, made these efforts difficult.

▼ Workers removing rubble after the attacks on the World Trade Center in New York City.

QUICK CHECK

Cause and Effect **Why did the United States send troops to Afghanistan?**

Check Understanding

1. **VOCABULARY** Write a sentence for each of the following words.

   treaty   annex

2. **READING SKILLS**
   Cause and Effect Use your chart from page 52 to write about wars Americans have fought.

Cause	→	Effect
	→	
	→	
	→	

3. **WRITE ABOUT IT** Write about the contributions of a person you read about in this lesson.

HISTORY of CANADA

VOCABULARY

Northwest Passage p. 62

voyageur p. 62

Loyalist p. 64

assembly p. 64

province p. 65

territory p. 65

READING SKILL

Cause and Effect

Fill in the chart with the causes and effects of European settlements in Canada.

Cause	→	Effect
	→	
	→	
	→	

New York Academic Content Standards

2.1, 2.2, 2.3, 2.4

On July 1, Canada Day, there are special celebrations with fireworks, picnics, and the Royal Canadian Mounted Police.

Visual Preview

How did Canada become a country of many cultures?

A First peoples of Canada include First Nations, Métis, and the Inuit.

B The French ruled New France for over 200 years.

C Canada came under British control in 1763.

D Millions of European immigrants settled in Canada.

Ⓐ NATIVE PEOPLES

Like the United States, Canada was once a colony of Great Britain. It is also a country of people with different backgrounds. But Canada's road to independence was much different from the road Americans chose.

Canada's indigenous people are known as First peoples. First peoples include First Nations, Métis, and the Inuit. First Nations are what is known in the United States as Native Americans. They include the Iroquois and other people of the eastern woodlands, buffalo hunters of the Plains, and salmon fishers of the Pacific Coast. The Métis people have a mixture of First Nations, French Canadian, English, and Scottish ancestors. Métis culture includes fiddle playing and a dance called jigging.

The Inuit

Another group of First Peoples, called the Inuit, came much later. They settled in the far North. They adapted to their environment by learning to hunt seals and walruses and to catch fish from the icy waters. On land they travel by dog sled. On the water they paddle single-person boats made of sealskin called kayaks.

Snow goggles ▼

The First Nations and Inuit invented objects such as canoes, snowshoes, snow goggles and a game called lacrosse. Today, lacrosse is Canada's official summer sport.

QUICK CHECK

Cause and Effect Why did the Inuit learn to hunt seals and walruses?

First peoples on a moose hunt ▶

B NEW FRANCE

In the 1490s, many Europeans believed there was a water route across North America to Asia. They called this shortcut to Asia the **Northwest Passage**. The search for the Northwest Passage brought explorers to North America. However, the Northwest Passage was not found. Instead, both England and France claimed areas of Canada. France claimed the area around the St. Lawrence River. This region was called New France.

EVENT

The first Europeans in the area that is Canada today were **Viking explorers** from Scandinavia who landed in about A.D. 1000. They lived for a while on the Newfoundland coast but eventually left without establishing permanent settlements.

Vikings in Newfoundland, 1000

The Fur Trade

French explorers, settlers, and missionaries founded several cities. The first was a trading post at Quebec. They traded with First Nations for beaver furs, which they sold in Europe for a lot of money.

▲ Beaver hats, such as this one, were popular in Europe.

◄ Voyageurs have become folk heroes in Canada.

The French fur traders were called **voyageurs**, which means "travelers" in French. They paddled their birch-bark canoes for 16 hours a day in rivers around the Great Lakes, sometimes singing as they went. They carried guns, kettles, fabrics, and other goods to trade for beaver furs. They worked for fur companies, which sold the furs in Europe to be made into hats. At the time, wearing a beaver fur hat was very popular in Europe.

France Battles Britain

During the 1600s and 1700s, the English and French fought each other for territory around the globe. In 1707 England and Scotland united to form Great Britain. This laid the foundation for the British Empire. While France ruled Canada, or New France, Britain controlled the 13 colonies to the South as well as the Hudson Bay.

The struggle for power between France and England spread to North America. This conflict, which lasted from 1754 to 1763, was called the Seven Years' War in Canada and

Britain. The French asked their First Nations allies for help in defeating the British. But warfare and diseases had killed most First Nations by this time. Of those who were left, most fought on the side of the French.

France Loses Canada

The French and their First Nation alliance lost the war. France and Britain signed the Treaty of Paris in 1763. This treaty not only ended the war, it also ended French control of Canada. Britain now controlled Canada and all French land east of the Mississippi. An English-speaking country now ruled a French-speaking one. How would the British govern their sixty thousand new subjects?

QUICK CHECK

Cause and Effect What was the effect of beaver hats being popular in Europe?

▲ James Wolfe led a surprise attack up the steep hillside below the Plains of Abraham, to fight the battle that won the Seven Years' War.

DataGraphic

Canada 1861 to 1921

Study the graph and the time line. Then answer the questions.

Population of Canada 1861–1921

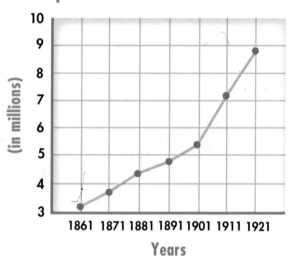

Events in Canada

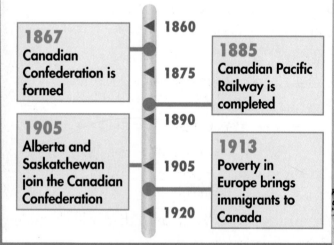

1867 Canadian Confederation is formed	1860
	1885 Canadian Pacific Railway is completed — 1875
	1890
1905 Alberta and Saskatchewan join the Canadian Confederation	1905
	1913 Poverty in Europe brings immigrants to Canada — 1920

Think About History

1. In which decade did population grow the most?

2. Why did Canada's population grow from 1911 to 1921?

In the 1500s, King Henry VIII of England banned Catholicism. Most people living in Canada were French-speaking Roman Catholics. Still, the British ruled according to British law and banned Catholicism. But by 1774, American colonists to the south were growing restless. Britain realized it would need the support of all Canadians if the Americans rebelled. It passed a law allowing the French to practice their religion and to keep their own laws for their businesses and daily lives.

British Settlers

After the American Revolution, the British population increased in Canada. About 50,000 **Loyalists**, American colonists who had remained loyal to Britain, fled to Canada. They set up farms along the Atlantic coast in what is now Ontario. French-speaking Canadians lived mostly in present-day Quebec. The Loyalists wanted their own government, so in 1791 the British divided Quebec into two colonies, Lower Canada and Upper Canada. Each had its own elected **assembly**, or group of people who make laws.

These American Loyalists draw lots for their land after arriving in Canada after the end of the American Revolution. ▼

Canadian leaders worked out the details of the new nation at a conference held in London, England, from December 1866 to March 1867.

Forming and Growing a Nation

Just as the United States gained its independence from Great Britain and grew from 13 states to 50, Canada also changed. It united, expanded, and gained its independence—only not quite the same way. Canada's changes were more gradual and more peaceful.

From 1791 to 1867, British North America was a collection of six separate colonies: Nova Scotia, New Brunswick, the Province of Canada (now Quebec and Ontario), Newfoundland, Prince Edward Island, and British Columbia. These colonies quarreled with each other over colonial government policies. Fears of being taken over by the United States, however, forced them together.

On July 1, 1867, the British North America Act united Quebec, Ontario, New Brunswick, and Nova Scotia into one nation. July 1 is now celebrated as Canada Day.

Other British-ruled areas—Manitoba, British Columbia, Saskatchewan, Alberta, Prince Edward Island, and Newfoundland— joined the nation later. Today, Canada is made up of 10 **provinces** and 3 additional **territories**—Yukon, the Northwest Territories, and Nunavut. A province is a division of a country, like a state. A territory is a part of a country that lacks the full rights of a province.

QUICK CHECK

Cause and Effect **How did the American Revolution cause an increase in Canada's British population?**

D EXPANSION AND INDEPENDENCE

Under Canada's central government, the colonies became provinces, much like states in the United States. Canada now had its own central government to run local affairs. Great Britain, though, still controlled Canada's relations with other countries.

Moving West

During the late 1800s, Canada expanded quickly. Pioneers traveled west across the plains and prairies. The Northwest Mounted Police (now the Royal Canadian Mounted Police) were founded to patrol the four western territories that joined Canada between 1870 and 1905. In 1885 the Canadian Pacific Railway linked east and west together. Soon hundreds of thousands of European immigrants were on their way to start farms on the mostly empty land west of Quebec. Almost two million more immigrants settled in cities such as Toronto and Montreal.

▼ After a potato famine in Ireland in the 1840s, over a million Irish people left Ireland for Canada and the United States. These Irish immigrants are arriving at Grosse Isle, Canada, on the St. Lawrence River.

Changes in Government

In 1982 Canadians peacefully won the right to change their constitution without British approval. Now fully independent, Canadians have to worry about the problem of being a nation divided by language. At Canada's founding, the government promised to protect Quebec's French language and culture. Many English-speaking Canadians did not keep this promise. As a result, many Québécois, as French-Canadians wish to be called, want to become a separate nation.

QUICK CHECK

Cause and Effect **What effect did the opening of the Canadian Pacific Railway have on western Canada?**

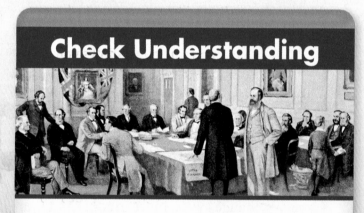

Check Understanding

1. **VOCABULARY** Write a paragraph about New France using these terms.

   Northwest Passage   **voyageur**

2. **READING SKILL Cause and Effect** Use the chart from page 60 to write about why Europeans settled Canada.

Cause	→	Effect
	→	
	→	
	→	

3. **WRITE ABOUT IT** Write about how the Seven Years' War changed Canada.

Map and Globe Skills

Use a Historical Map

VOCABULARY

historical map

In 1670 the Hudson Bay Company was granted a charter by King Charles II giving it all the rivers and streams flowing into the Hudson Bay. They named this territory Rupert's Land. In 1791 the British divided Quebec into two colonies, Lower Canada and Upper Canada. You can see these political changes by looking at a **historical map**. This kind of map shows information about the past or where events from the past took place.

Learn It

- Look at the map title and dates to find the map topic. This map shows you Canada in 1791. Most historical maps have dates.

- Look at the boundaries on a historical map. This will tell you about where settlements or events were located. The map on this page shows you where British colonies in Canada were located.

- Look at the map key to find the meaning of symbols or shading on the map. This will tell you about where settlements or events were located. The key on this map shows you lands that belonged to the British, Spanish, and the United States.

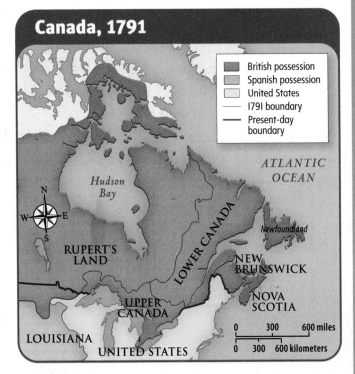

Canada, 1791

Legend:
- British possession
- Spanish possession
- United States
- 1791 boundary
- Present-day boundary

ATLANTIC OCEAN
Hudson Bay
RUPERT'S LAND
LOWER CANADA
Newfoundland
NEW BRUNSWICK
NOVA SCOTIA
UPPER CANADA
LOUISIANA
UNITED STATES

0   300   600 miles
0   300   600 kilometers

Try It

- Which part of present-day United States was part of Rupert's Land?

- Which color represents Spanish lands?

Apply It

- As you read the rest of this book, look for other historical maps.

- Compare the information that is given in those maps with the information that you read in each lesson.

Lesson 3

VOCABULARY

representative democracy p. 69

checks and balances p. 69

federalism p. 70

amendment p. 72

READING SKILL

Cause and Effect
Fill in the chart below with the causes and effects of dividing the powers of government.

Cause	→	Effect
	→	
	→	
	→	

New York Academic Content Standards
5.1, 5.2, 5.3, 5.4

UNITED STATES GOVERNMENT

The U.S. Capitol houses the legislative branch of the government.

Visual Preview

How does the U.S. Constitution affect citizens?

A The Constitution gives each branch of government its own powers.

B Power is divided between the federal and state governments.

C Citizens have rights and responsibilities.

D The Bill of Rights guarantees freedom and equal rights to all.

A THE U.S. CONSTITUTION

"We the People of the United States." These are the first words of the United States Constitution. What did the leaders of the new United States have in mind in 1787 when they wrote this government plan?

The United States is a **representative democracy**. This means that voters choose leaders who make and enforce the laws. The Constitution is the plan that sets up how our government works. The leaders who wrote it wanted a government strong enough to provide for the needs of its citizens. They also wanted a government with limited powers so it would not be able to take away people's rights.

Dividing Power

To achieve these goals, the writers of the Constitution divided the government's power among three branches: legislative, executive, and judicial. The two houses of Congress (House of Representatives and Senate) form the legislative branch. The President is the head of the executive branch. The Supreme Court and other national courts make up the judicial branch.

Each branch has its own powers and can limit the power of the other branches. This system is called **checks and balances**. It's a way to keep any one branch from becoming too powerful.

QUICK CHECK

Cause and Effect **Why is the power of the government divided among three branches?**

The original U.S. Constitution is in the National Archives in Washington, D.C. ▼

Checks and Balances

Legislative Branch	Executive Branch	Judicial Branch
• Congress (elected) • Passes laws • Approves taxes and spending • Can override vetoes	• President (elected) • Enforces laws • Commander-in-Chief of military • Signs or vetoes laws	• Supreme Court and federal courts (appointed) • Decides constitutional questions about laws

Ⓑ FEDERALISM

The principle of checks and balances also operates between the powers of the national government and the governments of the states. Our first leaders wanted to create a strong central government. They wanted state governments to have certain powers and responsibilities too.

The system they developed is called **federalism**. In federalism, power is divided between the federal, or national, government and the state governments. Some powers are given to the states. Others are given to the federal government. The chart below shows some of the rights and responsibilities of each.

QUICK CHECK

Cause and Effect Why did our first leaders develop federalism?

THE FEDERAL GOVERNMENT

- ▶ makes treaties with other countries
- ▶ has the power to make laws about trade between states
- ▶ declares war
- ▶ runs the post office
- ▶ mints money
- ▶ collects taxes

U.S. President
George W. Bush

STATE GOVERNMENTS

- ▶ sets up local governments
- ▶ makes laws about education
- ▶ makes laws about health
- ▶ sets up public schools
- ▶ runs local elections
- ▶ collects taxes

New York State Governor
David Paterson

▲ Immigrant members of the U.S. Navy become United States citizens

In the United States federal system, people are citizens of both the nation and their state. As a result, citizens have the right to vote for both national and state leaders. The U.S. Constitution and state constitutions give them that right. Citizens have the duty to make informed decisions when they vote. Citizens also have the responsibility to obey national and state laws.

QUICK CHECK

Cause and Effect How does the federal system affect the people of the United States?

Citizenship

Rights and Responsibilites

As an American citizen, you have the responsibility to protect not only your own rights, but the rights of others. Suppose you were asked to attend a meeting to suggest rules for the playground. You have a right to speak and give your suggestions. You also have a responsibility to be careful about what you say and to respect the ideas of others.

Write About It Explain the responsibilites citizens have when voting, and what might happen if people were not allowed to vote.

THE BILL OF RIGHTS

Individual freedom is a basic value of the United States. In 1791 ten **amendments**, or additions, known as the Bill of Rights were added to the U.S. Constitution. Their purpose was to prevent the government from taking away people's freedoms. The first amendment is the most famous and most important.

> **❝**Congress shall make no law respecting an establishment of religion, or prohibiting the free exercise thereof; or [limiting] the freedom of speech, or of the press; or the right of the people peaceably to assemble, and to [ask] the Government [to hear their complaints].**❞**

Among other things, this amendment guarantees that Americans can speak freely and can practice the religion of their choice.

Over the years, other amendments have been added. Equal rights is a basic value that has taken years to develop. The Constitution's 14th Amendment, added after the Civil War, guarantees all citizens the same legal rights.

Unequal Rights

Still, all Americans have not always enjoyed equal rights. Some groups have suffered unfair treatment. For several decades after independence, only white males could vote. African American males were guaranteed the right to vote when the 15th Amendment was added to the Constitution in 1870. Women could not vote across the country until the 19th Amendment was added in 1920. Today, many groups continue to fight for equal rights.

QUICK CHECK

Cause and Effect **What was the result of the Fourteenth Amendment to the Constitution?**

Check Understanding

1. **VOCABULARY** Write about the U.S. Constitution using these terms.

   representative democracy
   checks and balances

1. **READING SKILL** Cause and Effect Use your chart from page 68 to write about the U.S. Constitution.

Cause	→	Effect
	→	
	→	
	→	

3. **Write About It** Write about how the U.S. Constitution protects freedoms.

Members of the U.S. Senate at the Democratic National Convention in 2004. Ninety women were serving in the U.S. Congress in 2007. ▲

Chart and Graph Skills

Read Parallel Time Lines

VOCABULARY

time line
parallel time line

A **time line** is a diagram of events arranged in the order in which they took place. Sometimes time lines have a break in time that is shown with a symbol. The symbol means a period of years is not shown.

The time line below is a **parallel time line**. Parallel time lines show two sets of dates and events on the same time line. In the parallel time line below, events in United States history are shown at the top and amendments, or additions, to the U.S. Constitution are shown on the bottom.

Learn It

- Identify the years labeled on the time line. The time line below is labeled for every five years.

- Identify the events on a parallel time line.

- Compare the events on the top of the time line with the events on the bottom of the time line. Use the parallel time line to see what events happened at around the same time.

Try It

- Which amendment followed the election of Thomas Jefferson?

- Which two events happened at the same time on the parallel time line?

Apply It

- Which event led to the Fourteenth Amendment?

- Why do you think the Fifteenth Amendment was added?

United States Events

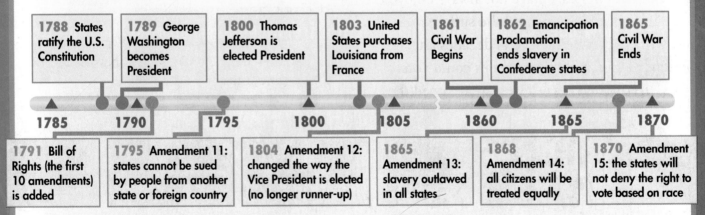

| 1788 States ratify the U.S. Constitution | 1789 George Washington becomes President | 1800 Thomas Jefferson is elected President | 1803 United States purchases Louisiana from France | 1861 Civil War Begins | 1862 Emancipation Proclamation ends slavery in Confederate states | 1865 Civil War Ends |

1785 **1790** **1795** **1800** **1805** **1860** **1865** **1870**

| 1791 Bill of Rights (the first 10 amendments) is added | 1795 Amendment 11: states cannot be sued by people from another state or foreign country | 1804 Amendment 12: changed the way the Vice President is elected (no longer runner-up) | 1865 Amendment 13: slavery outlawed in all states | 1868 Amendment 14: all citizens will be treated equally | 1870 Amendment 15: the states will not deny the right to vote based on race |

Amendments to the U.S. Constitution

Canada's Government

VOCABULARY

prime minister p. 75

parliament p. 75

monarch p. 75

READING SKILL

Cause and Effect

As you read, fill in the chart with the cause and effects of a parliamentary government.

Cause	→	Effect
	→	
	→	
	→	

New York Academic Content Standards
5.1, 5.4

The Peace Tower of the parliament building in Ottawa

Visual Preview

How does Canada's government differ from the government of the United States?

A Canada is an independent country but still honors the British queen.

B Parliament and a prime minister govern Canada.

THE CANADIAN CONSTITUTION

Canada is a democracy, just like the United States. Yet in some ways it is very different from the United States. Canada's Constitution was written in 1867 and 1982, and parts of it are unwritten customs.

Canada has a **prime minister**, who is the head of a democratic government, and a **parliament**. A parliament is an assembly of people who pass the laws governing a nation. Voters elect representatives to parliament. These representatives then choose a prime minister to head the government. The British **monarch**, the king or queen, serves as Canada's head of state. The head of state has ceremonial duties but no real power. Because the monarch visits Canada only once in a while, a Canadian official called the governor general serves as head of state.

Canada's Constitution

Canada's form of government is based on its Constitution. Unlike the U.S. Constitution, Canada's is not just one document. The Constitution Act of 1867 is part of it. So is the Constitution Act of 1982. Long-standing customs and principles make up the third, unwritten, part of the Constitution.

QUICK CHECK

Cause and Effect **How do Canadian voters affect the selection of the prime minister?**

Queen Elizabeth signs Canada's constitutional proclamation in Ottawa, Canada, on April 17, 1982. Prime Minister Pierre Trudeau, seated across from her, looks on.

B SIMILARITIES AND DIFFERENCES

Like the United States, Canada has a federal system. The federal government is in charge of matters that affect all of Canada. This includes making national laws, providing national defense, and setting foreign policies. Provincial and territorial governments are in charge of education, health care, and highways.

Unlike the United States, Canada does not have a complete separation of powers because the parliament chooses the prime minister. The prime minister depends on the support of parliament. If parliament stops supporting the prime minister and his or her policies, a new national election must be called.

HOW THE U. S. GOVERNMENT WORKS

- is a representative democracy
- the President is elected by voters through the Electoral College
- the President is the head of government and head of state
- the plan of the government is set out in the Constitution, a single document written in 1787
- the three branches of government check each other's powers
- has a federal system with power divided between the central government and the states
- has a Bill of Rights to protect the basic liberties of United States citizens
- Congress has two elected houses, the Senate and the House of Representatives

HOW CANADA'S GOVERNMENT WORKS

- is a parliamentary democracy
- members of parliament choose the prime minister
- the prime minister is the head of government and the British monarch is the head of state
- the plan of government is set out in the Constitution, several written Acts plus unwritten customs
- the prime minister depends on the support of parliament
- has a federal system with power divided between the central government and the provinces and territories
- has a Charter of Rights and Freedoms to protect the basic liberties of Canadian citizens
- Parliament has two houses, the Senate and the House of Commons; senators are appointed and members of the House of Commons are elected

Canadian Prime Minister Stephen Harper speaks to the House of Commons in Parliament ▲

The Charter of Rights and Freedoms

Canada's Charter of Rights and Freedoms lists people's rights. These include freedom of expression, conscience, religion, thought, belief, peaceful assembly and association. It also includes equal rights without regard to "race, national or ethnic origin, color, religion, sex, age or mental or physical disability."

Health Care

Unlike the United States, Canada pays for its citizens health care. Together, national and local governments pay for about 70 percent of Canadians' health costs, including almost 100 percent of hospital and doctor care.

QUICK CHECK

Compare and Contrast **How are the offices of president and prime minister alike and different?**

Check Understanding

1. **VOCABULARY** Write about Canada's government using the following terms.

   prime minister   **parliament**   **monarch**

2. **READING SKILL**
   Cause and Effect Use your chart from page 74 to write about Canada's parliamentary government.

Cause	→	Effect
	→	
	→	
	→	

3. **Write About It** Compare and contrast the U.S. government with the Canadian government.

Cultures and Lifestyles of the United States

VOCABULARY

rural p. 84

urban p. 84

suburb p. 84

READING SKILL

Cause and Effect

Copy the chart below. As you read, fill it in with the causes and effects of American diversity.

Cause	→	Effect
	→	
	→	
	→	

New York Academic Content Standards

1.1, 1.2, 1.3, 1.4, 2.1, 2.3

Independence Day is a national holiday that celebrates our country's Declaration of Independence, which was signed on July 4, 1776.

Visual Preview

How do people affect American life today?

A Many people speak Spanish, Chinese, Vietnamese, Italian, and German.

B The United States includes people of many different ethnic backgrounds.

C The arts reflect the American spirit and diversity.

D Most American families own their own homes.

Ⓐ DIVERSE TRADITIONS

Many different countries from around the world have contributed to American culture. Many of our foods, words, ideas, and traditions began in other countries. Yet, Americans have combined many of these traditions to make them a unique part of the spirit of America.

Most people in the United States have someone in their family background who was an immigrant. Over the years, people have come to the United States from just about every corner of the globe. This diversity is seen in many aspects of American culture.

Diversity in Language

In the United States, you can see the influence of different cultures everywhere. Spanish is the most widely spoken language after English. More than one million people speak Chinese, French, Vietnamese, Tagalog, German, and Italian. In fact, one out of six people in the United States speaks a language other than English as their first language.

Diversity in Religion

Religious life is also diverse. Most Americans are Christians, mainly Protestants. These groups vary widely in their beliefs and practices. Roman Catholics make up the next largest group of Christians, followed by the Eastern Orthodox. Judaism and Islam each have about 5 million followers in the United States. About 2 to 3 million Americans practice Buddhism, and another million are followers of Hinduism.

QUICK CHECK

Cause and Effect Why does the United States have such a diverse culture?

Chinese characters cover storefronts in Sunset Park, Brooklyn. ▶

A NATION OF IMMIGRANTS

The United States has been called a nation of immigrants. Immigrants are people who come from one country to another to live. Most immigrants to the United States came for a better life. The areas of the world contributing the most immigrants have changed over the years.

A Changing People

In the late 1700s and early 1800s, most Americans came from Great Britain. Other early European immigrants were the Germans and Scots-Irish. From the late 1800s to the 1920s, most immigrants came from southern, central, and eastern Europe.

1849 CALIFORNIA GOLD RUSH
Two years after gold was discovered, 25,000 Chinese immigrants came to the land they called Gold Mountain. In 1882 Congress passed a law blocking almost all immigration from China.

1808 IMPORTING SLAVES BANNED
Starting in 1619, most Africans came to America unwillingly as slaves.

1775   1825   1875

1845 IRISH POTATO FAMINE
The potato crop failed in Ireland. Within the next five years, over one-half million Irish people immigrated to America.

New Laws

In 1924 Congress passed a law keeping out immigrants from almost everywhere except northern and western Europe. In 1961 Congress passed a new law, basing entry into the United States on work skills and links to relatives, not on national origin.

QUICK CHECK

Cause and Effect **How did the 1961 Immigration Law affect the pattern of immigration?**

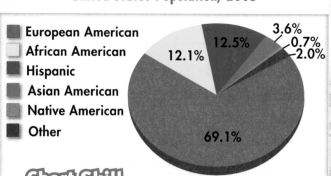

United States Population, 2005

- European American
- African American
- Hispanic
- Asian American
- Native American
- Other

3.6%
0.7%
2.0%
12.5%
12.1%
69.1%

Chart Skill

What percentage of the U.S. population in 2006 was Hispanic?

1892 ELLIS ISLAND OPENS

During the next forty years, 12 million immigrants, including millions of Italians, Poles, Russians, and Greeks, passed through Ellis Island in New York Harbor.

2000 A NEW CENTURY

Because of new laws and economic and political conditions worldwide, the number of immigrants to the United States rose during the late 1900s. Of these immigrants, nearly half came from the Americas. Another third came from Asia. Less than 15 percent came from Europe.

1925   **1975**   **2025**

1959 REVOLUTION IN CUBA

When Fidel Castro took over Cuba, hundreds of thousands of Cubans fled to Miami.

American artists have their own unique American styles. Painters are often inspired by the American landscape. Winslow Homer painted the stormy waters of the North Atlantic. Georgia O'Keeffe painted the colorful deserts of the Southwest. Thomas Eakins and John Sloan often painted the gritty side of city life. The earliest American artists used materials from their environments to create works of art. For centuries, Native Americans have carved wooden masks or made beautiful designs on pottery from clay found in their areas.

Literature

Many writers write about the human condition, or experience, in their region of the country. Mark Twain's books tell about life along the Mississippi River in the mid-1800s. Nathaniel Hawthorne wrote about the people of New England. Willa Cather and Laura Ingalls Wilder showed the struggles people faced settling the Great Plains. William Faulkner wrote about life in the South.

Other writers write about the unique experience of a group of people. The poetry of Langston Hughes and the novels

LAURA INGALLS WILDER
Little House on the Prairie
65th Anniversary
ILLUSTRATED BY GARTH WILLIAMS

Georgia O'Keeffe ▶

▲ Pueblo potter

◀ Langston Hughes

▼ Kyung-Wha Chung

▲ Dizzy Gillespie

▲ Lion King director Julie Taymor

of Toni Morrison portray the triumphs and sorrows of African Americans. The novels of Amy Tan examine the lives of Chinese Americans. Oscar Hijuelos and Sandra Cisneros write about the country's Latinos.

Music and Film

Americans have created unique musical styles. Country music grew out of folk music from the rural South in the 1920s. It gained many fans as it developed over the following decades. In the early 1900s, African Americans like Louis Armstrong, Ella Fitzgerald, and Dizzy Gillespie developed blues and jazz. Blues later inspired rock and roll in the 1950s. Recently, rap and hip-hop have gained popularity.

Immigrants have enriched American musical life, such as the violinist Kyung-Wha Chung, who immigrated from Korea when she was 13.

New Yorkers and visitors enjoy Broadway theater. Musicals like *Beauty and the Beast* and *The Lion King* are especially popular with young people. In the early 1900s, movies started attracting large audiences. Today, the movie industry continues to make movies that are popular with audiences worldwide. After 1950 television became a major part of American culture.

QUICK CHECK

Cause and Effect **What does the diversity of American art and literature reflect?**

DAILY LIFE

Daily life for Americans has always been active. Before the Industrial Revolution, the United States was made up entirely of **rural**, or country, areas. At that time, people did so much work, they often turned work into a game, such as corn husking contests. Now, the country is primarily a land of **urban**, or city, dwellers. To find more room to live, Americans moved from cities to **suburbs**, or smaller communities surrounding a larger city.

Since the 1970s, the fastest-growing areas in the country have been in the South and Southwest—often called the Sunbelt because of their sunny, mild climates.

Ways of Life

Lifestyles vary across the United States. For example, Americans live in a variety of different types of houses, from one-story ranch houses in suburbs to high-rise apartments in cities. About two-thirds of all American families own their own homes, one of the highest rates in the world. This is because of the high incomes of average U.S. workers compared to workers in the rest of the world. The United States also has high rates of car ownership. In addition, the United States is the leading country in ownership of personal computers and in Internet use.

While many Americans enjoy watching movies, television, and sports, many are also very active. They exercise and play sports such as golf, racquetball, tennis, softball, and bowling. Millions of young Americans take part in youth sports leagues, playing sports such as baseball and soccer.

▼ Sun City is a suburb of Phoenix, Arizona.

▲ Many Americans own their own homes.

Soccer is a popular sport in the United States.

Holidays

Some American holidays, like Martin Luther King, Jr.'s, birthday and President's Day, celebrate American heroes. Thanksgiving and the Fourth of July are other holidays Americans celebrate nationwide. Some holidays, like St. Patrick's Day and Cinco de Mayo, honor diverse religious and ethnic traditions.

QUICK CHECK

Cause and Effect **Why do so many American families own their own homes?**

Check Understanding

1. **VOCABULARY** Use the following words to write the opening paragraph of a magazine article.

   rural   urban   suburbs

2. **READING SKILL** Cause and Effect Use your chart from page 78 to write about American diversity

Cause	→	Effect
	→	
	→	
	→	

 EXPLORE The Big Idea

3. **Write About It** Write about a unique characteristic of your community.

VOCABULARY

bilingual p. 87

multiculturalism p. 87

separatism p. 88

READING SKILL

Cause and Effect

Copy the chart below. As you read, fill it in with the causes and effects of separatism in Canada.

Cause	→	Effect
	→	
	→	
	→	

New York Academic Content Standards

2.1, 2.2, 3.1

Cultures and Lifestyles of Canada

Canadian women's ice hockey team celebrates at the Olympic Winter Games in Torino, 2006

Visual Preview

How do people make living in Canada unique?

A People of different backgrounds live in Canada.

B Parts of Canada want to govern themselves, including the Inuit in Nunavut.

C Canada has a rich culture of literature, music, and film.

D Canadians enjoy sports and other outdoor activities.

Ⓐ A MIX OF CULTURES

If you went to a hockey game in Toronto, Canada, fans would sing the country's national anthem "O Canada," in English. If you went to a hockey game in Montreal, you would hear the same song in French.

As you read in Lesson 2, the French set up trading posts in Canada during the 1600s. As a result of the Seven Years' War, the British won control of Canada in 1763. Now Canada is a **bilingual** country. Bilingual means "two languages." Canada has two official languages—English and French. Canada has adopted **multiculturalism** as an official policy. Most Canadians are proud of being part of a country that not only accepts but celebrates differences.

▲ A First Nations wood-carver.

The People of Canada

Canada has 33 million people. About one-fourth have French ancestry and live mainly in Quebec. Another fourth have British ancestry. They live mainly in Ontario, the Atlantic Provinces, and British Columbia.

Like the United States, Canada is a nation formed by immigrants with many different cultures. After the French and British, people of other European ancestry form about 15 percent of the population. Canada also is home to people of Asian, African, and Latin American backgrounds. First Nations make up more than a million people. Most First Nations live on reserves, or land set aside for indigenous people. If you were to visit one of Canada's 2,200 reserves, you would find that many Indians living there continue to follow traditional ways of life.

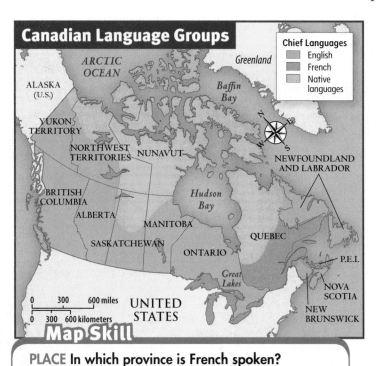

Canadian Language Groups

Chief Languages
- English
- French
- Native languages

ARCTIC OCEAN

Greenland

ALASKA (U.S.)

Baffin Bay

YUKON TERRITORY

NORTHWEST TERRITORIES   NUNAVUT

NEWFOUNDLAND AND LABRADOR

BRITISH COLUMBIA

Hudson Bay

ALBERTA

MANITOBA

SASKATCHEWAN

ONTARIO

QUEBEC

P.E.I.

Great Lakes

NOVA SCOTIA

NEW BRUNSWICK

0   300   600 miles
0   300   600 kilometers

UNITED STATES

Map Skill

PLACE **In which province is French spoken?**

QUICK CHECK

Cause and Effect **Why is Canada a bilingual country?**

Over the years, Canadians in some provinces have promoted the idea of **separatism**, or independence from the rest of Canada. This idea is strongest in the province of Quebec.

Separatist Quebec

Quebec is the largest province in area. French-speaking people make up about 80 percent of its population. Many French speakers in Quebec do not believe that their language and culture can survive in largely English-speaking Canada. They would like Quebec to separate from Canada and set up an independent government while still maintaining certain economic ties. Others believe Quebec should remain part of Canada. So far, the separatists have been defeated in two very important votes on this issue.

The Quebec flag ▲

Western Canada

In 2005 a study found that over 35 percent of the people in Canada's western provinces—British Columbia, Saskatchewan, and Manitoba—also want to separate from the rest of Canada. These westerners feel they do not have much in common with eastern Canadians.

This feeling is especially strong in Alberta. Plans for separation differ. Some people want Alberta to be completely independent. Some want it to join with other western provinces to form one nation. Others would like it to become the 51st state of the United States.

As in Quebec, all of these plans have so far been defeated. Canada's future as a united country, however, is still uncertain.

PLACES

Quebec City is the capital of the province of Quebec. It is one of the oldest cities in North America. The walls that once protected it still exist.

Quebec City

This Montreal stop sign is in French and English. ▼

ARRÊT
STOP

Snowmobile race in
the Northwest Territories ▲

The town of Pangnirtung on Baffin Island in Nunavut ▼

Nunavut

For many years, the Inuit, a northern native people who live in the Northwest Territories, demanded a return of some of their native lands. They wanted to rule themselves while remaining part of Canada. The Canadian government finally agreed. In 1999 Nunavut was carved out of the Northwest Territories. Nunavut means "Our Land" in the Inuit language, the official language of the territory. Although the largest territory of the country, it has the fewest people. Only about 30,000 people live in an area the size of Western Europe. If it were a country, it would be the 13th largest country in the world, with the fewest people per square mile.

In the past, most Inuit survived by hunting and fishing. Today, the Inuit work in businesses and industries. These include mining, oil and gas, construction, real estate, tourism, and government services. About 30 percent work, at least part of the time, as artists—sculpting, carving, and making prints. Inuit artists are known worldwide. Some Inuit continue to hunt part-time. They enjoy snowmobiling and other cold-weather sports. In 2002 Iqualit, the capital of Nunavut, was co-host for the Arctic Winter Games.

QUICK CHECK

Cause and Effect **What was the result of the Inuit's demand for a return of their land?**

Today, Canadian art reflects both European and native influences. The first Canadian artists were First peoples who carved figures from bone, stone, and wood. They also made pottery and wove baskets. The beauty of Canada's landscape has been a favorite subject for artists like Emily Carr. Nature and history have been popular subjects for Canadian writers. *Anne of Green Gables* by Lucy Maud

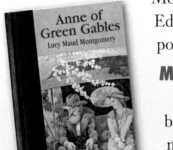

Montgomery, the story of a Prince Edward Island orphan, has been popular for one hundred years.

Music

For centuries, First peoples have been enjoying song, dance, and mime. Irish ballads and Scottish tunes were popular after the 1700s. In recent decades, pop and rock have become popular in Canada.

Houses by the Sea by modern artist Joy Anson ▲

A scene from *The Merchant of Venice* by Shakespeare at the Stratford Festival in Stratford, Ontario ▲

Skidegate, Graham Island, British Columbia, 1928, by Emily Carr ▶

Theater and Film

Movies are a big part of Canadian culture. The nation's film industry earns $5 billion a year. Many American films are made in Toronto and Vancouver. Theater is popular too. Ontario's Stratford Festival is known for its productions of William Shakespeare's plays. Some Canadian stars, like singer Celine Dion and actor Jim Carrey, are world famous. Canada's Cirque du Soleil, French for "Circus of the Sun," travels all over the world.

QUICK CHECK

Compare and Contrast Why is Canadian art similar to art in the United States?

Singer Celine Dion

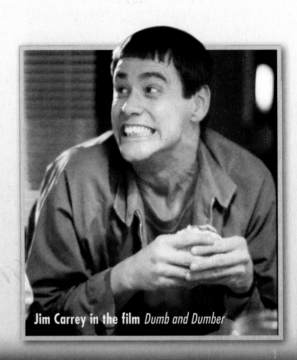

Jim Carrey in the film *Dumb and Dumber*

Montreal-based Cirque du Soleil is a circus with no animals, no understandable language, and no average clowns. ▼

D LIFE IN CANADA

Canada has welcomed many immigrant families to its shores over the years. These families have kept many of the customs of their homelands.

Favorite Foods

If you were to walk down a street in Toronto, you would likely see restaurants that feature Italian or Eastern European foods. This is a result of the immigrant groups who settled there. Certain foods are favorites in some regions of Canada. For example, fish, chowder, and oysters are popular in the Atlantic Provinces. French cuisine, such as chicken simmered in wine, is preferred in Quebec. People in British Columbia and Vancouver often eat salmon and Asian food.

Sports and Holidays

Canadians are huge hockey fans. Hockey, the national sport, was invented in Canada. Another sport with a long tradition in Canada is lacrosse, which was originally a First peoples game. Many Canadians enjoy outdoor activities such as skiing, boating, hunting, and fishing.

Canadians celebrate many holidays throughout the year. Canada Day, on July 1, celebrates the forming of their nation. The fall harvest holiday of Thanksgiving is celebrated on the second Monday of October. Canada's war dead are remembered on Remembrance Day, November 11. The current monarch's birthday is celebrated on Victoria Day.

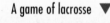

A game of lacrosse ▼

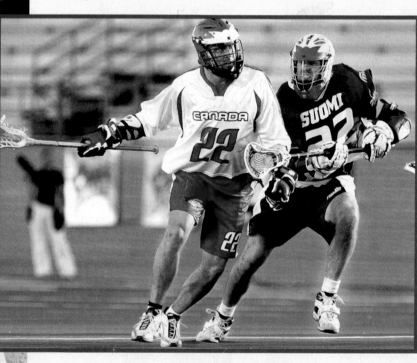

◄ A fish market in Vancouver, British Columbia

Ice skating in Ottawa

The Royal Canadian Mounted Police on Canada Day ▲

The Royal Canadian Mounted Police

The Mounties, as the Royal Canadian Mounted Police are called, are one of Canada's best-known symbols. They are the national police force. They also police most of the provinces and territories.

Originally, the Mounties were called the North West Mounted Police. They were formed in the late 1800s to bring law and order to the North-West Territories, Canada's own "wild west." Today the Mounties guard the prime minister and other government figures, police urban and rural areas, enforce federal laws, and protect against terrorists.

The Mounties began to accept women in 1974. The first all-woman troop graduated the next year. In 2006 Commissioner Beverley A. Busson became the top officer in the force.

QUICK CHECK

Cause and Effect Why does Toronto have Italian and East European restaurants?

Check Understanding

1. **VOCABULARY** Use the words below to write the first paragraph of a magazine article about Canada today.

   multiculturalism   **bilingual**

2. **READING SKILL Cause and Effect** Use your chart from page 86 to write about separatism in Canada.

Cause	→	Effect
	→	
	→	
	→	

3. **Write About It** Write about a unique characteristic of life in Canada.

Vocabulary Review

Number a paper from 1 to 4. Beside each number write the word from the list below that matches the description.

treaty   amendment

assembly   separatism

1. the idea of independence from a country

2. an addition to the U.S. Constitution

3. an agreement between two or more countries

4. a group of people who make laws

Comprehension and Critical Thinking

5. Why did colonists fight for independence from Great Britain?

6. What was President Lincoln's Emancipation Proclamation?

7. Reading Skill What caused Britain to divide Canada into Lower Canada and Upper Canada in 1791?

8. Critical Thinking Why did Loyalists flee to Canada after the American Revolution?

Skill

Use a Historical Map

Write a complete sentence to answer each question.

9. Which land in North America did France control in 1763?

10. Which country claimed Louisiana in 1763?

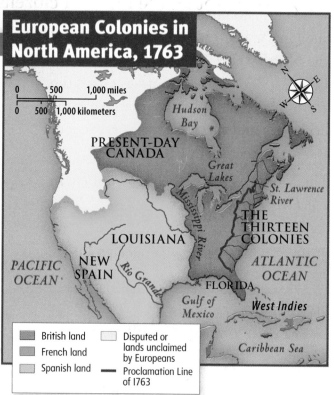

European Colonies in North America, 1763

0 500 1,000 miles
0 500 1,000 kilometers

Hudson Bay

PRESENT-DAY CANADA

Great Lakes

St. Lawrence River

Mississippi River

THE THIRTEEN COLONIES

LOUISIANA

PACIFIC OCEAN

NEW SPAIN

Rio Grande

ATLANTIC OCEAN

FLORIDA

Gulf of Mexico

West Indies

Caribbean Sea

British land
French land
Spanish land
Disputed or lands unclaimed by Europeans
— Proclamation Line of 1763

New York Social Studies Test Preparation

Base your answers to question 1 through 3 on the passage below and on your knowledge of social studies.

Citizens of the United States have rights guaranteed by the Bill of Rights. These are the first ten amendments to the United States Constitution. For example, we can talk freely about our ideas and practice any religion. American citizens also have responsibilities, such as voting, following the laws, and paying taxes.

Source: James A. Banks, et al., *New York,* Macmillan/McGraw-Hill, 2007

1 What are some freedoms of citizens of the United States?

Write your answer on a separate piece of paper.

Score

2 What are some responsibilities of citizens of the United States?

Write your answer on a separate piece of paper.

Score

3 What guarantees the rights of citizens of the United States?

Write your answer on a separate piece of paper.

Score

The Big Idea Activities

How do people affect the history and culture of a region?

Write About the Big Idea

A Descriptive Journal Entry
Use the Unit 2 Foldable to help you write a descriptive journal entry that answers the Big Idea question, *How do people affect the history and culture of a region?* Use the notes you wrote under each tab in the Foldable for details to support each main idea. Begin with an introduction. In the body of the entry, be sure to include the cause and effect of the topic you chose to write about. End with a conclusion about how people affect a region.

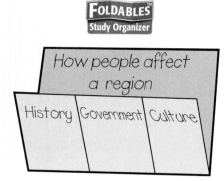

FOLDABLES Study Organizer

How people affect a region

History | Government | Culture

Unit 2 Activity

Work with a partner to make a parallel time line. Place Canadian events on the top of your time line and U.S. events on the bottom.

1. Decide what period in history your time line will include.

2. Research events during that time at the library or on the Internet.

3. Illustrate your time line with drawings or photos of the events.

When you have finished your parallel time line, take turns explaining each event on your time line to the class.

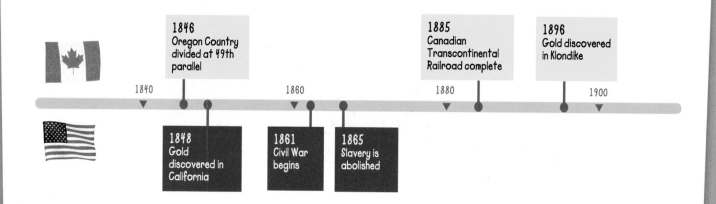

1846 Oregon Country divided at 49th parallel

1885 Canadian Transcontinental Railroad complete

1896 Gold discovered in Klondike

1840   1860   1880   1900

1848 Gold discovered in California

1861 Civil War begins

1865 Slavery is abolished

Unit 3

EXPLORE The Big Idea

Essential Question
How does the economy affect people's lives?

FOLDABLES™ Study Organizer

Make Generalizations
Make and label an envelope Foldable before you read Unit 3. Write on the tabs: **Free Enterprise**, **Knowledge Economy**, **Free Trade**, and **Environment**. Use the Foldable to organize information as you read.

LOG ON For more about the United States and Canada today, go to www.macmillanmh.com

The Ambassador Bridge links Detroit, Michigan, in the United States with Windsor, Ontario, in Canada

THE UNITED STATES AND CANADA TODAY

PEOPLE, PLACES, AND EVENTS

Alexander Graham Bell

Rachel Carson

Beinn Bhreagh, Nova Scotia

1907 | Bell forms the Aerial Experiment Association

Springdale, Pennsylvania

1962 | Carson's book, *Silent Spring*, is published

1875   1900   1925

Alexander Graham Bell formed the Aerial Experiment Association to develop the first plane to fly in Canada.

Today his home, where he formed the association and got many of his best ideas, is still standing in **Beinn Bhreagh, Nova Scotia**.

Rachel Carson wrote to warn of the dangers of using certain chemicals to kill pests.

Today you can see the Sense of Wonder Garden, an organic garden of native plants, at the Rachel Carson Homestead in **Springdale, Pennsylvania**.

Bill Gates

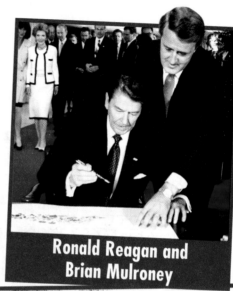
Ronald Reagan and Brian Mulroney

Microsoft Redmond Campus

1975 | Gates founds Microsoft

Palm Springs, California

1988 | Canada–U.S. Free Trade Agreement is signed

1950   1975   2000

Bill Gates was still in college when he and a friend developed the first computer language program for a personal computer.

Today you can tour the **Microsoft Redmond Campus** near Seattle, Washington.

The **Canada–U.S. Free Trade Agreement** was signed in the desert town of **Palm Springs**, **California**.

Today you can visit Palm Springs, where winter temperatures average above 70 degrees.

Economic Regions of the United States

The trading floor of the New York Stock Exchange

VOCABULARY

free enterprise p. 101

stock p. 101

profit p. 101

biotechnology p. 102

supply p. 104

demand p. 104

READING SKILL

Make Generalizations
Copy the chart below. As you read, use it to make a generalization about free enterprise.

Text Clues	What You Know	Generalization

New York Academic Content Standards
3.1, 4.1, 4.2

Visual Preview

How does the United States economy work?

A People decide what to make, how much to make, and how much to charge.

B The Northeast and Midwest have cities with large and small businesses.

C Prices of some products in the South are affected by supply and demand.

D Diverse industries thrive in the Interior West and Pacific regions.

(A) FREE ENTERPRISE

*The United States has a **free enterprise** system. In a free enterprise system, people can start any business they want. They decide what to make, how much to produce, and what price to charge.*

Goods and services vary throughout the United States. Geographers group states into five economic regions—the Northeast, the Midwest, the South, the Interior West, and the Pacific. All of these regions practice free enterprise, also known as capitalism.

Stocks and Profits

Under free enterprise and capitalism, people are free to risk their savings in a business. People invest in companies by buying **stock**. Stock is part ownership in a company. When a company makes money, it often pays some of this money to people who own stock. If the business fails, however, the stock becomes worthless.

Profit is the amount of money left over after all the costs of production have been paid. Profit is often the measure stock-buyers use to determine how well a company is doing. The profit motive is the driving force that encourages companies and individuals to improve their wealth. Profit motive is largely responsible for the growth of a free enterprise system based on capitalism. "Capitalism is this wonderful thing that motivates people, it

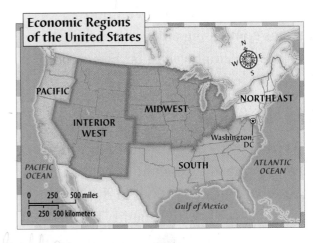

Economic Regions of the United States

causes wonderful inventions to be done," said Bill Gates, the founder of Microsoft.

Voluntary exchange is part of capitalism. It occurs when buyers and sellers make a market trade with anyone they chose. Voluntary exchange is a way for us to improve our well-being.

QUICK CHECK

Make Generalizations **How does voluntary exchange improve our well-being?**

Shopping is part of the free enterprise system ▶

Every economic region must answer the question: what goods and services will be produced and in what amount? Two economic regions, the Northeast and the Midwest, answer that question by looking at their resources. Both regions contain big cities where skilled workers are employed in businesses both large and small.

PLACES

In 1790 the **NYSE** began on Wall Street in New York City. Today it is the largest stock exchange in the world in terms of dollars traded.

NY Stock Exchange

The Northeast

With few mineral resources and poor soil for farming in many areas, the Northeast has long focused on business. Cities in the Northeast include New York, the country's largest city, and Washington, D.C., the nation's capital. The federal government is responsible for about 50 percent of the jobs in Washington. New York has many financial and media, or communications, companies. Most stocks traded in the United States are traded on the New York Stock Exchange (NYSE), the American Stock Exchange, or an electronic stock market like the NASDAQ. Boston is an important center of **biotechnology** research. Biotechnology is the study of cells to find ways of improving health. Philadelphia's economy is heavily based upon manufacturing and financial services.

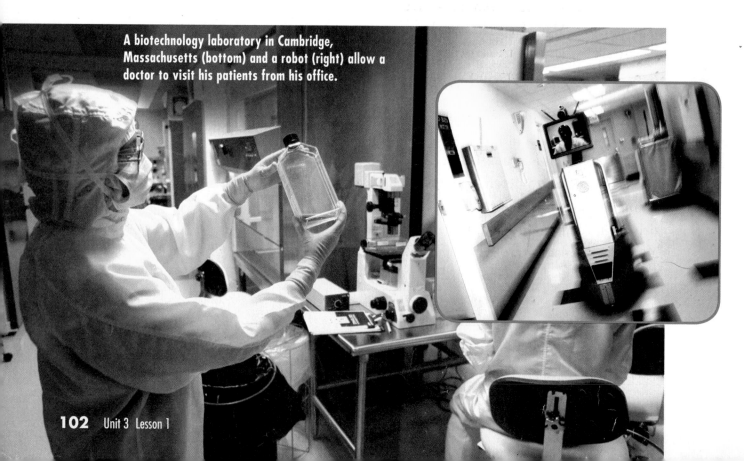

A biotechnology laboratory in Cambridge, Massachusetts (bottom) and a robot (right) allow a doctor to visit his patients from his office.

In 2001, this aid cargo plane from Chicago helped earthquake survivors in India. ▶

The Midwest

Unlike the Northeast, the Midwest has plenty of fertile, or rich, soil. Midwestern farmers grow corn, wheat, soybeans, and other crops. Farms are bigger than they were fifty years ago, but there are fewer farmers. Only a small percentage of farms are owned by corporations, but these farms are extremely large. Farming can be a difficult business. High costs, unpredictable weather, hard and time-consuming work add to its difficulty. Advances in technology have made farming easier. But these new machines are expensive. Small family farmers may not be able to afford the technology they need to make a profit.

The Midwest is also rich in mineral resources. These include iron ore, coal, lead, and zinc. Since the 1800s, these resources have fueled manufacturing. Manufacturing has been an important source of jobs in the cities of the Midwest. Detroit excelled in automobiles and Cleveland in steel. New technology, however, has led to the decline of older industries. As a result, the Midwest now focuses on other industries, such as telecommunications. Chicago, for example, has the third largest economy in the United States. More and more companies are moving to the Chicago area to take advantage of the city's central location for shipping goods. Chicago has the second largest workforce in the United States.

QUICK CHECK

Make Generalizations **Why are companies moving to Chicago?**

A Detroit automaker displaying an electric hybrid car in 2007 ▲

C THE SOUTH

All markets have a buying side and a selling side. The prices of oil and cotton, for example, are determined by **supply** and **demand**. Supply is the amount of a product or service that producers are willing to sell at all possible market prices. Demand is the opposite of supply. Buyers demand different amounts of a good or service depending on the price that sellers ask. Producers offer different amounts of a product or service depending on the price that buyers are willing to pay.

The South's economy has a long history of being affected by these market pressures. Texas, Louisiana, and Alabama have long been producers of oil. When the supply of oil is low and the demand is high, the price tends to go

THEN

Fifty years ago, many people in the South worked on small family farms. Family farms were passed down from generation to generation. Most everything people needed to live was grown or raised on the family farm.

In the 1900s, it became profitable for companies to manufacture textiles (or cloth) in southern states where cotton was grown, winters were mild, and heating costs were low. Many Southerners worked in mill towns, or towns that grew up around textiles factories.

up. When the demand for oil is low and the supply is high, the prices tend to go down. In 1986 the price of oil dropped so low that many people in the South lost their jobs.

In recent decades, however, the South has changed rapidly. Today, the area has expanding cities, growing industries, and diverse populations. Workers in cities such as Houston, Dallas, and Atlanta make textiles, electrical equipment, computers, and airplane parts. Florida relies on tourism and trade with Latin America that flows through the port of Miami. Northern Virginia, near Washington, D.C., is now a telecommunications center. North Carolina is one of the South's largest centers for biotechnology research.

QUICK CHECK

Make Generalizations **Make a generalization about effects of supply and demand.**

NOW

Today, many Southerners work in high-tech environments such as North Carolina's Research Triangle Park, the largest research park in the world. Along with research parks in Virginia and Alabama, the "New South" is home to global scientific centers.

The economy of the South is booming in all areas of technology including telecommunications, information technology, software development, biotechnology, and aerospace technology. The Northern Virginia Technology Council is the largest technology council in the nation.

The Interior West and Pacific have long struggled with the question: how shall goods and services be produced? Because both areas are mainly arid, they often suffer from droughts. Most of the people in these regions depend on irrigation to keep their economies alive.

The Rugged Interior West

The magnificent mountains and plateaus of the Interior West draw many people. Grasses thrive in certain places, and where the land is irrigated, you find agriculture. For many decades, mining, ranching, and lumbering have been the Interior West's main economic activities. In recent years, other parts of the area's economy have grown rapidly. The cities of Denver and Salt Lake City both have growing information technology industries. Service industries are important to Albuquerque and Phoenix, two cities that attract many tourists each year.

Tourists in New Mexico buying Navajo crafts ▼

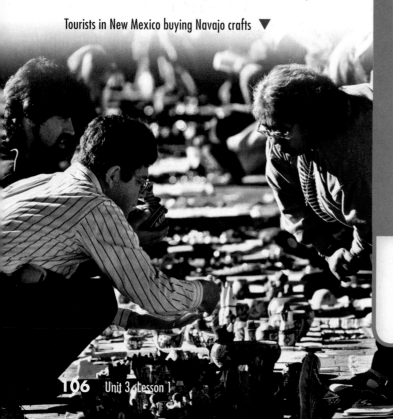

DataGraphic
The United States Economy

The graph shows how the U.S. economy is divided by category. The map shows the location of selected industries. Study the graph and map. Then answer the questions below.

United States Economy, 2006

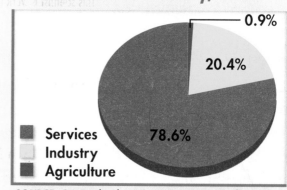

- 0.9%
- 20.4%
- 78.6%

■ Services
■ Industry
■ Agriculture

SOURCE: CIA Factbook, 2006   *Percentages are rounded

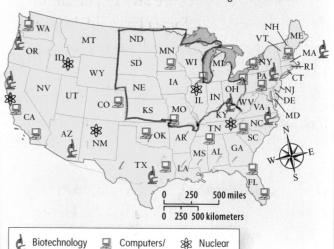

🔬 Biotechnology   💻 Computers/Electronics   ⚛ Nuclear research

Think About the U.S. Economy

1. What is the largest part of the U.S. economy?

2. Which states have nuclear research?

This worker is studying a magnified diagram of a computer microchip.

This scientist is working with a new kind of tiny robot called a "nanobot." ▲

The Diverse Pacific

The Pacific area includes the western coastal states plus Alaska and Hawaii. Farmers raise fruits and vegetables in the fertile valleys of California, Oregon, and Washington. Sugarcane, pineapples, and coffee are grown in the rich volcanic soil of Hawaii. Fish, timber, and mineral resources are also important in the Pacific area. California has gold, lead, and copper. Alaska has vast reserves of oil, and large timber and fishing industries.

Many diverse industries thrive in the Pacific area. Workers in California and Washington make airplanes and develop computer software. The city of Los Angeles is the world center of the movie industry. Tourism is also a large source of income. California has the largest economy and population in the United States. It also has great ethnic diversity. Nearly half of its people are Latino or Asian American.

Check Understanding

1. **VOCABULARY** Write a paragraph about the U.S. economy using these words.

   stock   supply
   profit   demand

2. **READING SKILLS** Make Generalizations Use your chart from page 100 to write about free enterprise.

Text Clues	What You Know	Generalization

3. **Write About It** Explain how supply and demand affect the price of goods.

QUICK CHECK

Make Generalizations **Make a generalization about the Pacific economy.**

ECONOMIC REGIONS of CANADA

VOCABULARY

developed nation p. 109

economic growth p. 109

knowledge economy p. 111

READING SKILL

Make Generalizations
Copy the chart below. As you read, use it to make a generalization about Ontario's economy.

Text Clues	What You Know	Generalization

New York Academic Content Standards
3.1, 4.1, 4.2

A wood chip pile at a paper mill in British Columbia

Visual Preview

How do the regions of Canada affect its economy?

A Industries in the Atlantic provinces have grown Canada's economy.

B Ontario is responsible for 40 percent of Canada's economic growth.

C British Columbia's forests make Canada the largest producer of paper.

D Diamond mines in the Northwest Territories make this region wealthy.

A ATLANTIC PROVINCES

*Like the United States, Canada is a **developed nation**. This means it has a high level of economic development and its economy includes high technology, services, manufacturing, and extraction (such as mining).*

Developed nations also have a high average income per person. Other developed nations include Japan, Australia, and the countries of Western Europe. Like the United States, Canada consists of different economic regions. It also has a free enterprise economy in which people start and run businesses with limited government involvement.

Economic Growth

Canada's economy has changed over the years. Fishing was a major industry in the Atlantic provinces of Newfoundland and Labrador, Nova Scotia, Prince Edward Island, and New Brunswick. Offshore waters, however, have become overfished. Now, few people there make their living from the sea. Instead, the Atlantic provinces's manufacturing, mining, and tourism industries have experienced **economic growth**. Economic growth is an economy's increase in the value of goods and service. This growth has made the city of Halifax, Nova Scotia, a major shipping port.

Canada's government plays a role in its economic growth.

Fish-processing workers in Atlantic Canada ▶

PEOPLE

In 1961 Tommy Douglas led a movement that brought medical care to every Canadian citizen. Today he is known as the "father of Medicare."

Tommy Douglas

For example, Canada's national and provincial governments provide health care for citizens. Broadcasting, transportation, and electric power companies are government-supported. These public services might not have been available in Canada's remote areas without government support.

QUICK CHECK

Make Generalizations **How has Canada's fishing industry changed?**

Because Canada produces many more goods than it can use, it needed to answer the question: for whom shall goods and services be produced? Canada turned to other countries to sell its goods and services, especially to the United States. About 85 percent of Canada's exports are sold to the United States. Canada's central province, Ontario, exports the most.

Ontario's Wealth

Ontario has the most people and greatest wealth of Canada's provinces. It is responsible for over 40 percent of Canada's annual economic growth and is the largest industrialized area in Canada. Manufacturing is the main industry in this region. Ontario has excellent transportation links to the American heartland and the Great Lakes. This means exports can travel easily by land or by water.

Ontario's major products include motor vehicles, iron, steel, food, electrical appliances, machinery, chemicals, and paper. Ontario surpassed Michigan in car production in 2004. It is also a major area for agricultural, forestry, and mining.

Ontario's capital, Toronto, is Canada's largest city and a major banking and business center. Due to recent immigration, Toronto's workforce today comes from 170 countries.

Hydroelectric power plant in Quebec ▼

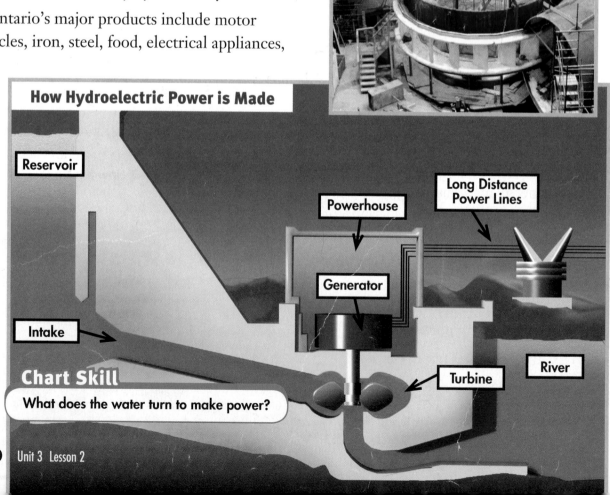

How Hydroelectric Power is Made

Reservoir

Powerhouse

Long Distance Power Lines

Generator

Intake

Chart Skill

What does the water turn to make power?

Turbine

River

Hydroelectric Power

Ontario's half of the Niagara Falls makes it ideal for producing hydroelectric energy. Hydroelectric power accounts for 30 percent of the province's energy needs. To understand how hydroelectric energy is produced, look at the diagram on page 110. Because of Ontario's large manufacturing industries, the province has been forced in recent years to purchase power from other areas. As a result, Quebec and Michigan have sold power to Ontario during its peak power periods.

Fertile Quebec

East of Ontario is the Canadian province of Quebec. In southern Quebec, the St. Lawrence River Valley is a fertile agricultural region. It produces dairy products, fruits, vegetables, and livestock. Quebec is also the largest producer of maple syrup.

North of the St. Lawrence River Valley, Quebec is extremely rich in its forest, lake, and river resources. Paper, lumber, and hydroelectric power are some of the province's most important industries.

A Knowledge Economy

While Quebec's natural resources are important to its economy, Montreal, Quebec's largest city, has a different economy. Montreal has a **knowledge economy**.

These aerospace workers are putting together a jet engine in Montreal ▲

A knowledge economy makes a profit on the production and management of information. Knowledge economies include industries such as biotechnology, information and communication technologies, and aerospace, or companies that make aircraft. In fact, Montreal is the world's fourth largest producer of aircraft.

Alexander Graham Bell invented an important part of communication technology—the telephone. He lived the second half of his life in Beinn Bhreagh, Nova Scotia. There he set up the original Bell Laboratory. The laboratory conducted experiments and built kits and airplanes. During World War I, it built lifeboats for the Canadian navy.

QUICK CHECK

Make Generalizations Make a generalization about a knowledge economy.

◄ Canada's National Tower in Toronto is the tallest structure in the world.

THE WEST

The west economic region of Canada includes the Prairie Provinces of central Canada and British Columbia on the Pacific coast. There, agriculture and mining are important industries.

The Prairie Provinces

In the Prairie Provinces of Manitoba, Saskatchewan, and Alberta, farming and ranching make up the main economy. This area produces large amounts of wheat for export and contains some of the world's largest reserves of oil and natural gas.

British Columbia

The province of British Columbia on the Pacific coast has extensive forests. They help make Canada the world's largest producer of newsprint, the type of paper used for printing

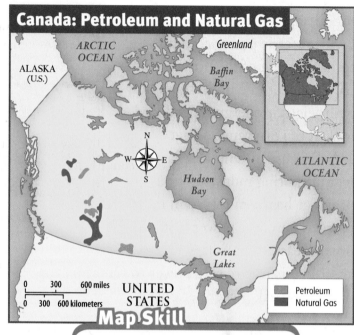

Canada: Petroleum and Natural Gas

Legend: Petroleum, Natural Gas

Map Skill

REGION Which region has the largest petroleum deposit?

newspapers. Timber, mining, fishing, and tourism also support British Columbia's economy.

A Canadian forest ranger

QUICK CHECK

Make Generalizations **Make a generalization about Canada's forests.**

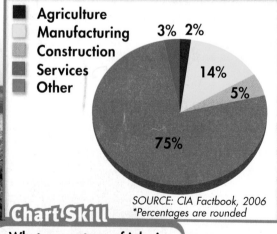

Jobs in Canada

Legend:
- Agriculture
- Manufacturing
- Construction
- Services
- Other

3% 2%
14%
5%
75%

SOURCE: CIA Factbook, 2006
*Percentages are rounded

Chart Skill

What percentage of jobs in Canada are in construction?

D THE NORTH

Canada's vast north covers about one-third of the country. This area includes the territories of Yukon, the Northwest Territories, and Nunavut. Many of the 25,000 people in this region are indigenous peoples. The main resources in the North are minerals, such as gold and diamonds. Diamond mines make the Northwest Territories one of the wealthiest regions in the world.

In the Yukon territory, manufacturing includes furniture, clothing, and handicrafts. Hydroelectricity is also produced. The traditional industries of trapping and fishing have declined. Today, the government is by far the biggest employer in the territory. It directly employs about 5,000 of its 12,500-person workforce.

QUICK CHECK

Make Generalizations **Why are the Northwest Territories wealthy?**

▼ A Yukon gold mine

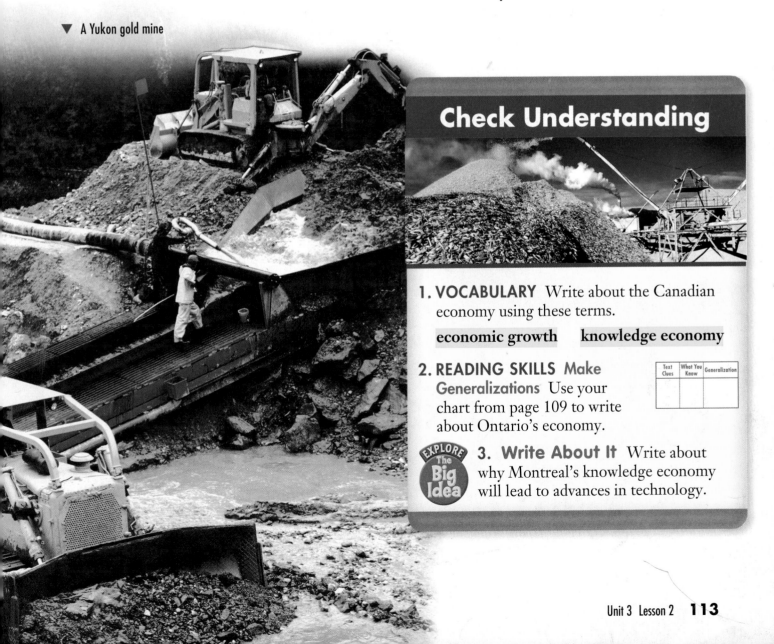

Check Understanding

1. **VOCABULARY** Write about the Canadian economy using these terms.

   economic growth   knowledge economy

2. **READING SKILLS** Make Generalizations Use your chart from page 109 to write about Ontario's economy.

Text Clues	What You Know	Generalization

3. **Write About It** Write about why Montreal's knowledge economy will lead to advances in technology.

Lesson 3

VOCABULARY

interdependence p. 115

FTA p. 115

tariff p. 115

trade deficit p. 116

trade surplus p. 116

READING SKILL

Make Generalizations
Copy the chart below. As you read, use it to make a generalization about the relationship between the United States and Canada.

Text Clues	What You Know	Generalization

New York Academic Content Standards
4.1, 4.2

The United States, Canada, and the World

World leaders gather in Alberta, Canada, to discuss global issues.

Visual Preview

How do Canada and the United States cooperate?

A Canada and the United States trade goods with each other and the world.

B Canada and the U.S. provide much of the money that funds the UN.

C Canada sent troops to protect the Afghanistan capital of Kabul.

A   ECONOMIC TIES

In many ways, the economies of the world's countries are tied together.
Trade allows countries to export goods and raw materials.
It also allows them to import goods and materials they need.
The United States and Canada depend on trade for economic growth.

Global **interdependence**, or dependence on each other to meet needs and wants, allows countries to specialize in certain products and materials. Trade agreements help countries do business. The Canada–U.S. Free Trade Agreement (FTA) is one example. In 1988 Canada and the United States signed this agreement, which ended trade barriers between the two nations.

Free Trade

Since the trade agreement, Canada and the United States have increased the value of the goods they ship to each other. Free trade, or trade without **tariffs** has helped the United States and Canada build stronger economies. Tariffs are taxes on goods brought into a country. Because of global trade, Americans and Canadians enjoy goods from all over the world, and products from both countries are used throughout the world. This trade creates jobs for American and Canadian workers. Canada is now the largest trading partner of the United States, and Mexico is the second largest.

QUICK CHECK

Make Generalizations **Make a generalization about global interdependence.**

The Port of Vancouver ▼

DIFFERENCES AND COOPERATION

The United States and Canada have economic differences. While both countries rely on trade for economic growth, the United States also depends on trade for energy resources. Americans use three times the amount of oil our country produces. We must therefore import additional oil from countries such as Canada, Mexico, Venezuela, Saudi Arabia, and Nigeria.

Economic Differences

The value of a country's money is affected by the nation's balance of trade. Balance of trade is the difference between the value of a nation's exports and its imports. The United States spends more on imports than it earns from exports. The resulting **trade deficit**, or when the value of a country's imports is higher than its exports, is hundreds of billions of dollars.

Canada, by contrast, enjoys a **trade surplus**, that is, it earns more from exports than it spends for imports. Canada's export earnings have grown yearly at a higher rate than those of the United States.

Military Cooperation

The United States and Canada have been close military allies since 1940. They share an active military exchange program between the two countries during times of war. For example, Canadian navy ships train together with the U.S. Navy battle groups. The Canadian military has fought alongside the United States in most major wars since World War II. Most recently, Canadian forces have helped the United States in the Iraq War.

Value of US Imports and Exports

Source: U.S. Department of Commerce

Imports
Exports

Chart Skill

In which year is the trade deficit the largest?

Primary Sources

When we work together as countries to make North America safer and more competitive, then the fact is all of the continent and all of our citizens benefit from that collective achievement.

Section from a speech by Prime Minister Paul Martin, March 23, 2005

Write About It Write about why all citizens benefit from collective achievement.

The United States and Canada also have strong roles in the United Nations. They provided much of the money that funds the organization. They also take part in UN agencies that provide aid to people in areas affected by war or natural disasters. The United States and Canada have also sent soldiers to serve in UN forces that act as peacekeepers in troubled areas of the world.

QUICK CHECK

Make Generalizations **Why does the United States have a large trade deficit?**

The United Nations headquarters in New York City ▼

Citizenship

Cooperation and Compromise

When the United States and Canada agreed on the FTA, they were using cooperation and compromise. People use cooperation when they work together to make rules or laws, or solve a problem. People compromise when they give up a part of something they want. By getting along and working together, everyone contributes to a solution that everybody can live with.

Write About It Write a paragraph about a time you gave up something you wanted to solve a problem or settle a disagreement.

C WAR ON TERROR

American life changed dramatically on September 11, 2001 when terrorists crashed passenger planes into buildings. About 3,000 people died in the attacks. To prevent further terrorist attacks, the United States and Canada have worked to increase security along their long border. They also have participated in international efforts to stop terrorism.

In 2001 United States troops invaded the country of Afghanistan in Southwest Asia. Afghanistan's rulers, known as the Taliban, had protected the terrorist group al Qaeda. The Taliban were forced from power; however, many terrorists escaped. In 2002 Canada sent troops in support of a United Nations effort to protect Kabul, the capital of Afghanistan.

QUICK CHECK

Make Generalizations Make a generalization about why you think the Taliban wanted to protect al Qaeda.

Check Understanding

1. **VOCABULARY** Write about Canadian and U.S. trade using these terms.

   trade deficit

   trade surplus

2. **READING STRATEGY Make Generalizations** Use your chart from page 114 to help you write about the relationship between the United States and Canada.

Text Clues	What You Know	Generalization

3. **Write About It** Write about why Canada and the United States signed a free trade agreement.

EXPLORE The Big Idea

Afghan children receiving school supplies from Canadian soldiers ▶

Map and Globe Skills

Compare Maps at Different Scales

VOCABULARY

map scale

small-scale map

large-scale map

All maps are drawn to scale. A **map scale** uses a unit of measurement, such as an inch, to show distance on Earth. A map scale explains the size of the area on a map.

A **small-scale map**, such as Map A, shows a large area, but cannot include many details. A **large-scale map**, such as Map B, shows a smaller area with more details.

Learn It

- If you want to find out where Albany is located, use a small-scale map, or Map A. It has a scale of 80 miles.

- If you want to know the location of Goat Island, you would need the large-scale map, or Map B. It has a scale of 0.25 miles and shows more details, such as streets.

- Compare the scales of both maps.

Map A: New York State

Try It

- Which map would you use to find the distance between Rochester and Niagara Falls?

- Which map would you use to find the location of streets near Niagara Falls?

Apply It

- Compare a map of the United States with a map of New York.

- Compare the map scales. Is the state map a large- or small-scale map?

Map B: Niagara Falls

Lesson 4

VOCABULARY

fossil fuel p. 121

acid rain p. 121

conservation p. 121

urbanization p. 124

urban sprawl p. 124

READING SKILL

Make Generalizations

Copy the chart below. As you read, use it to make a generalization about deforestation.

Text Clues	What You Know	Generalization

New York Academic Content Standards

3.1, 3.2

Environmental Issues

Under these protective caps are cedar saplings that are part of the reforestation of British Columbia.

How does the economy affect the environment?

A The burning of fossil fuels to make energy pollutes our environment.

B Deforestation increases the level of carbon dioxide, which leads to global warming.

C Urban sprawl reduces farmland and wilderness areas.

A   THE PROBLEM OF POLLUTION

Environmentalist Rachel Carson said, "the present century has one species—man—[who has] significant power to [change] the nature of his world." But is there a solution to the problem of pollution?

To save the environment, countries around the world must work to end pollution. The United States and Canada have formed a group of scientists to find solutions to the problem of pollution.

Acid Rain

People in the United States and Canada burn **fossil fuels**—coal, oil, and natural gas—to power their factories and run their cars. Burning these fuels pollutes the air, endangering all who breathe it. Pollution from factories and cars also dissolve in rainwater to form **acid rain**, or rain containing high amounts of harmful chemicals. Acid rain has harmed forests and killed fish in lakes in some areas of the United States and Canada. An important way to reduce pollution is through **conservation**. Conservation is the protection and careful use of natural resources. Conservation limits the use of fossil fuels and restores our forests.

QUICK CHECK

Make Generalizations **How can people in the United States and Canada reduce pollution?**

A United States oil refinery polluting the air ▼

IMPACT ON THE ENVIRONMENT

While people fight the effects of acid rain on land, our oceans are also at risk. Spills from tanker ships have spread millions of gallons of oil onto beaches, killing fish, seabirds, and food for marine life.

Another environmental impact is deforestation. Deforestation is the removal of trees. Some trees are removed to create farmland. Others are removed in logging or to make room for growing cities. But trees naturally protect the environment. They absorb a greenhouse gas called carbon dioxide.

Carbon dioxide occurs naturally, but it has been increasing steadily since the Industrial

The deforestation of clearcut forest in Oregon contributes to higher carbon dioxide levels, which leads to global warming.

Hurricane Wilma flooded Pembroke Pines, Florida, in 2005 with 125 mile per hour winds that knocked down power lines and left millions without power.

Revolution with the burning of fossil fuels. At high levels, carbon dioxide contributes to the greenhouse effect, or global warming. Most scientists say that global warming will lead to a change in weather patterns. Hurricanes could become more severe. In some places, a warmer climate could lead to droughts. Increasing temperatures could melt the polar ice caps. This would cause flooding for low-lying areas.

The United States and Canada have passed laws to lower the amount of fossil fuels that are burned. They have also funded research to find cleaner sources of energy.

QUICK CHECK

Make Generalizations **What can high levels of carbon dioxide do to the environment?**

Workers clean oil from a beach after an oil tanker ruptured, spilling 39,000 gallons of oil in Dutch Harbor, Alaska, in 1997.

Rescue workers clean oil off the feathers of a black scoter duck caught in an oil spill in 1995.

Before and After

A lifeless urban street before it is turned into a social and economic center

The same neighborhood after investment shows walkable streets and an economic center

In 1800 about 5 percent of Americans lived in cities. Today, 80 percent of Americans live in cities. This change from rural to city living is called **urbanization**. During the Industrial Revolution, cities became the ideal place to locate factories and their workers.

Whereas urbanization helped fuel the Industrial Revolution, **urban sprawl** has created another challenge. Urban sprawl is the spread of human settlement into natural areas. It can lead to the loss of farmland and wilderness areas. The building of homes and roadways also produces traffic jams and more air pollution. At the same time, many Americans still have the dream of owning their own home. Their desire to fulfill that dream will probably spur continued building.

QUICK CHECK

Make Generalizations **What causes urban sprawl?**

Check Understanding

1. **VOCABULARY** Write a paragraph about pollution using these terms.

   fossil fuel   **acid rain**

2. **READING STRATEGY** Make Generalizations Use your chart from page 120 to write about deforestation.

Text Clues	What You Know	Generalization

3. **Write About It** Write about the effects of automobile technology on the environment.

Chart and Graph Skills

Compare Line and Circle Graphs

VOCABULARY

line graph
circle graph

Carbon dioxide is a harmful greenhouse gas. At high levels, greenhouse gases cause global warming. One way to measure carbon dioxide is to use **line graphs** and **circle graphs**. A line graph shows a change over time. A circle graph shows how something can be divided into parts. All of the parts together make up a circle. Circle graphs are also called pie graphs because the parts look like slices of a pie.

Learn It

● To find out what information a graph contains, look at its title.

● Study the labels on a graph. Labels on a line graph appear along the bottom of the graph and along the left side. Labels on a circle graph explain the subject.

Try It

● Look at the line graph. What was the global carbon dioxide level in 1950?

● Look at the circle graph. What source of carbon dioxide produces the highest levels in the United States?

Apply It

● Summarize the line graph's information about carbon dioxide.

● Summarize the circle graph's information about carbon dioxide.

● Summarize what both graphs tell you about global warming.

Global Carbon Dioxide Emissions

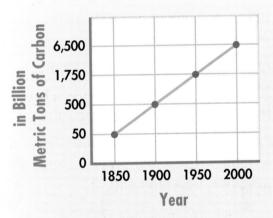

Source: World Resources Institute

U.S. Carbon Dioxide Emissions

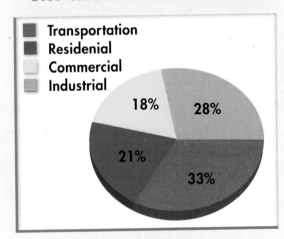

■ Transportation
■ Residenial
■ Commercial
■ Industrial

Source: Environmental Protection Agency

Unit 3 Review and Assess

Vocabulary Review

Number a paper from 1 to 4. Beside each number write the word from the list below that matches the description.

biotechnology   **tariff**

developed nation   **urban sprawl**

1. the spread of human settlements into natural areas

2. a fee or tax placed on goods that are brought into a country

3. the study of cells to find ways of improving health

4. a country with a high level of economic development

Comprehension and Critical Thinking

5. How does capitalism motivate people?

6. Why does the United States have a trade deficit?

7. **Reading Skill** What effect does acid rain have on the environment?

8. **Critical Thinking** Why does free trade lead to economic growth?

Skill

Compare Maps at Different Scales

Write a complete sentence to answer each question.

9. Compare the map on this page to the map of the New York on page 119. Is the map on this page a small-scale or a large-scale map?

10. About how many miles long is Manhattan on each of the maps?

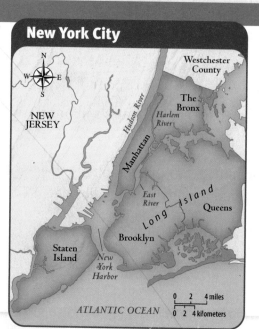

New York City

New York Social Studies Test Preparation

Base your answers to questions 1 through 3 on the line graph below.

Canadian Automotive Imports and Exports

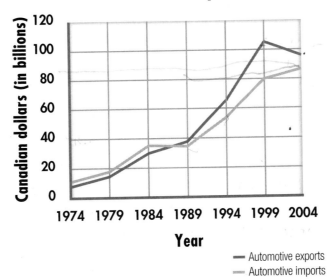

— Automotive exports
— Automotive imports

1 In which years were imports more than exports?

(A) 1974–1982
(B) 1988–1990
(C) 1990–1992
(D) 1994–2004

2 What was the amount of imports in 2004?

(A) about 60 billion
(B) about 75 billion
(C) about 80 billion
(D) about 95 billion

3 By how much did exports increase between 1994 and 1999?

(A) about 20 billion
(B) about 25 billion
(C) about 30 billion
(D) about 35 billion

How does the economy affect people's lives?

Write About the Big Idea

An Expository Essay

Use the Unit 3 Foldable to help you write an expository essay that answers the Big Idea question, *How does the economy affect people's lives?* Use the notes you wrote under each tab in the Foldable for details to support each main idea. Be sure to begin with an introduction that includes facts. Include one paragraph that explains the reason for each fact. End with a paragraph that makes a generalization about how the economy affects people's lives.

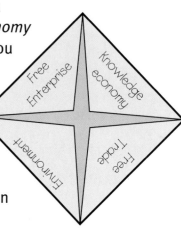

Make a Map of Forest Biotechnology

Forest biotechnology looks at ways to improve the health of forests by studying the cells of trees. Laboratory experiments include the study of tree cells and finding ways to modify the cells in laboratories. Field experiments include the actual study of forests and cell-modified trees in forests.

Work with a partner to make a map of forest biotechnology activity in the Western Hemisphere.

1. Draw an outline map of North and South America.

2. Use the information below to color your map.

Laboratory Experiments	Argentina, Mexico
Field Experiments	Canada, Chile, Brazil, and U.S.

3. Be sure to include a map key and title. You may also illustrate your map.

When you have finished your map, take turns presenting it to the class.

Reference Section

The Reference Section is a collection of tools that can be used to help you understand the information you read in this textbook.

Unit 1 • Reading Skills

Compare and Contrast

When you compare you notice how things are alike. When you contrast you notice how they are different. Comparing and contrasting will help you understand the people and events you read about in social studies.

Learn It

- To compare two things, note how they are similar. The words *alike*, *same*, and *both* are clues to similarities.

- To contrast two things, note how they are different. The words *different, however,* and *by contrast* show differences.

- Now read the passage below. Think about how you would compare and contrast farming in Canada and the United States.

Farming in Canada and the United States

Rich soil in parts of the United States and Canada help farmers grow crops. Canada's heartland is known as the "Prairie Provinces." It includes Manitoba, Saskatchewan, and Alberta. Wheat is the major farm crop in this region. In the area along the St. Lawrence Seaway, dairy farms produce products that are important to the economy.

Compare
This sentence shows how both countries are alike

Like Canada, farmers in the U.S. Midwest grow wheat and produce dairy products. However, the South's warm, wet climate favors crops that are not grown in Canada, such as rice and sugarcane.

Contrast
This tells how the countries are different

Try It

Copy the Venn diagram. Then fill in the left-hand side with Canadian farming activities. Fill in the right-hand side with American farming activities. Fill in the center with farming activities that both countries do.

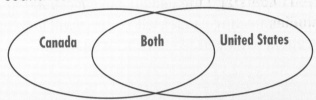

Canada   Both   United States

How did you figure out the similarities and differences?

Apply It

- Review the steps for comparing and contrasting in Learn It.

- Read the passage below. Use a Venn diagram to show the similarities and differences between the mineral resources of Canada and the United States.

The United States and Canada have vast mineral resources. A mineral is a natural substance that is found in the earth. Minerals have helped create industries in the United States and Canada.

Parts of eastern Canada and the northern United States both have large iron-ore deposits. Iron ore is used to make steel. The Rocky Mountains have gold, silver, and copper. Products made from copper include wire, pipes, and frying pans. Deep within the Canadian Shield are iron ore, copper, nickel, and gold. In fact, the shield supplies Canada with so many different minerals that it is often called "Canada's Storehouse."

The Canadian Shield

Unit 2 • Reading Skills

Cause and Effect

A cause is a person or event that makes something else happen. An effect is the result of the cause. When one event causes another event to happen, the two events have a cause-and-effect relationship. Connecting causes with effects will help you understand more about what you read in social studies.

Learn It

- After you finish reading a section, ask yourself, "What happened?" The answer to that question will help you identify an effect.

- Then ask yourself "Why did that happen?" The answer to this question helps you identify a cause.

- Look for the clue words *because, so,* and *as a result.* These words point to cause-and-effect relationships.

- Now read the passage below. Use the steps above to pick out cause-and-effect relationships.

Cause
This is a cause. It tells why.

Effect
This is an effect. It tells what happened.

Cause and Effect
This has a cause and an effect.

The American Revolution

The people in Great Britain's 13 colonies soon grew angry over British taxes and trade policies. In 1776 the colonists declared their independence from Great Britain. But Great Britain would not give up its colonies without a fight.

The Americans fought back and won several battles. The Revolutionary War lasted eight long years. Finally, in 1783 the United States won the war and Britain recognized American independence. A new nation called the United States was born.

Copy and complete the cause and effect chart below. Then fill in the chart with another cause and effect from the paragraph.

Cause →	Effect
→	
→	
→	

How did you figure out the causes and effects?

Apply It

● Review the steps for understanding cause and effect in Learn It.

● Read the passage below. Then use a chart to list the causes and effects from the passage.

After the American Revolution, the British population increased in Canada. About 50,000 Loyalists, American colonists who had remained loyal to Britain, fled to Canada. They set up farms along the Atlantic coast and in what is now Ontario. French-speaking Canadians lived mostly in present-day Quebec. The Loyalists wanted their own government, so in 1791 the British divided Quebec into two colonies, Lower Canada and Upper Canada. Each had its own elected assembly, or group of people who make laws.

Make Generalizations

When you read, sometimes it helps to make a generalization. A generalization is a broad statement that shows how different facts, people, or events have something in common. Being able to make generalizations will help you uncover similarities that you might otherwise not notice. Generalizations can also help you make sense of new information you will learn later.

Learn It

- Identify text clues with similarities or relationships.

- Apply what you already know about the topic.

- Make a generalization that is true about all of your text clues and what you know.

- Read the passage below. Think about a generalization you could make.

Text Clue
Imports and exports have increased.

Text Clue
Free trade builds stronger economies.

Text Clue
More choice in the goods we buy.

Canada–U.S. Free Trade Agreement

Since the Canada–U.S. Free Trade Agreement, Canada and the United States have increased the value of the goods they ship to each other. Free trade, or trade without tariffs (taxes on goods brought into a country), has helped the United States and Canada build stronger economies. Because of global trade, Americans and Canadians enjoy goods from all over the world, and products from both countries are used throughout the world.

Try It

Copy and complete the generalization chart below. Then make a generalization about free trade.

Text Clues	What You Know	Generalization

How did you figure out how to make a generalization?

Apply It

- Review the steps to make a generalization in Learn It.
- Read the paragraph below. Then make a generalization about pollution using a generalization chart.

People in the United States and Canada burn fossil fuels—coal, oil, and natural gas—to power their factories and run their cars. Burning these fuels pollutes the air, endangering all who breathe it. Chemicals from factories and cars also dissolve in rainwater to form acid rain, or rain containing high amounts of harmful chemicals. Acid rain has harmed forests and killed fish in lakes in some areas of the United States and Canada. An important way to reduce pollution is through conservation. Conservation is the protection and careful use of natural resources. Conservation limits the use of fossil fuels and restores our forests.

Geography Handbook

Geography and You

Many people think geography means learning about the location of cities, states, and countries, but geography is much more than that. Geography is the study of our Earth and all its people. Geography includes learning about bodies of water such as oceans, lakes, and rivers. Geography helps us learn about landforms such as plains and mountains. Geography also helps us learn about using land and water wisely.

People are an important part of the study of geography. Geography includes the study of how people adapt to live in new places. How people move, how they transport goods, and how ideas travel from place to place are also parts of geography.

In fact, geography has so many parts that geographers have divided the information into smaller groups to help people understand its ideas. These groups are called the six elements of geography.

Six Elements of Geography

The World in Spatial Terms: Where is a place located, and what land or water features does that place have?

Places and Regions: What is special about a place, and what makes it different from other places?

Physical Systems: What has shaped the land and climate of a place, and how does this affect the plants, animals, and people there?

Human Systems: How do people, ideas, and goods move from place to place?

Environment and Society: How have people changed the land and water of a place, and how have land and water affected the people who live in a place?

Uses of Geography: How has geography influenced events in the past, and how will it influence events now and in the future?

Five Themes of Geography

You have read about the six elements of geography. The five themes of geography are another way of dividing the ideas of geography. The themes, or topics, are **location**, **place**, **region**, **movement**, and **human interaction**. Using these five themes is another way to understand events you read about in this book.

1. Location

The White House

In geography, *location* means an exact spot on the planet. A location is usually a street name and number. You write a location when you address a letter.

2. Place

The Grand Canyon

A *place* is described by its physical features, such as rivers, mountains, or valleys. Human features, such as cities, language, and traditions can also describe a place.

3. Region

Wheat field in the Midwest

A *region* is larger than a place or location. The people in a region are affected by landforms. Their region has typical jobs and customs. For example, the fertile soil of the Mississippi lowlands helps farmers in the region grow crops.

4. Movement

Passenger train

Throughout history, people have moved to find better land or a better life. Geographers study why these *movements* occurred. They also study how people's movements have changed a region.

5. Human Interaction

Hoover Dam

Geographers study the ways that people adapt to their environment. Geographers also study how people change their environment. The *interaction* between people and their environment explains how land is used.

Dictionary of Geographic Terms

1 BASIN A bowl-shaped landform surrounded by higher land

2 BAY Part of an ocean or lake that extends deeply into the land

3 CANAL A channel built to carry water for irrigation or transportation

4 CANYON A deep, narrow valley with steep sides

5 COAST The land along an ocean

6 DAM A wall built across a river, creating a lake that stores water

7 DELTA Land made of soil left behind as a river drains into a larger body of water

8 DESERT A dry environment with few plants and animals

9 FAULT The border between two of the plates that make up Earth's crust

10 GLACIER A huge sheet of ice that moves slowly across the land

11 GULF Part of an ocean that extends into the land; larger than a bay

12 HARBOR A sheltered place along a coast where boats dock safely

13 HILL A rounded, raised landform; not as high as a mountain

14 ISLAND A body of land completely surrounded by water

15 LAKE A body of water completely surrounded by land

16 MESA A hill with a flat top; smaller than a plateau

17 **MOUNTAIN** A high landform with steep sides; higher than a hill

18 **MOUNTAIN PASS** A narrow gap through a mountain range

19 **MOUTH** The place where a river empties into a larger body of water

20 **OCEAN** A large body of salt water; oceans cover much of Earth's surface

21 **PENINSULA** A body of land nearly surrounded by water

22 **PLAIN** A large area of nearly flat land

23 **PLATEAU** A high, flat area that rises steeply above the surrounding land

24 **PORT** A place where ships load and unload their goods

25 **RESERVOIR** A natural or artificial lake used to store water

26 **RIVER** A large stream that empties into another body of water

27 **SOURCE** The starting point of a river

28 **VALLEY** An area of low land between hills or mountains

29 **VOLCANO** An opening in Earth's surface through which hot rock and ash are forced out

30 **WATERFALL** A flow of water falling vertically

Reviewing Geography Skills

Read a Map

Maps are drawings of places on Earth. Most maps have standard features to help you read the map. Some important information you get from a map is direction. The main directions are north, south, east, and west. These are called cardinal directions.

The areas between the cardinal directions are called intermediate directions. These are northeast, southeast, southwest, and northwest. You use these directions to describe one place in relation to another.

In what direction is Iowa from North Carolina?

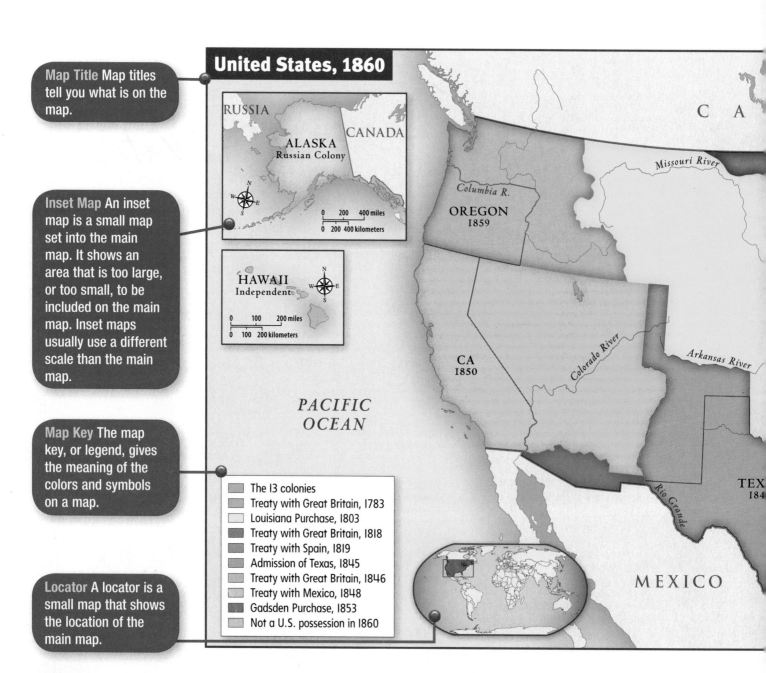

Map Title Map titles tell you what is on the map.

Inset Map An inset map is a small map set into the main map. It shows an area that is too large, or too small, to be included on the main map. Inset maps usually use a different scale than the main map.

Map Key The map key, or legend, gives the meaning of the colors and symbols on a map.

Locator A locator is a small map that shows the location of the main map.

United States, 1860

RUSSIA

ALASKA
Russian Colony

CANADA

0   200   400 miles
0   200   400 kilometers

HAWAII
Independent

0   100   200 miles
0   100   200 kilometers

PACIFIC OCEAN

C A

Missouri River

Columbia R.

OREGON
1859

CA
1850

Colorado River

Arkansas River

Rio Grande

TEX
184

MEXICO

The 13 colonies
Treaty with Great Britain, 1783
Louisiana Purchase, 1803
Treaty with Great Britain, 1818
Treaty with Spain, 1819
Admission of Texas, 1845
Treaty with Great Britain, 1846
Treaty with Mexico, 1848
Gadsden Purchase, 1853
Not a U.S. possession in 1860

Read Historical Maps

Some maps capture a period in time. These are called historical maps. They show information about past events or places. For example, this map shows the United States in 1860 just before the beginning of the Civil War. Read the title and the key to understand the information on the map.

What year did California become a state?

Which states entered the Union after California?

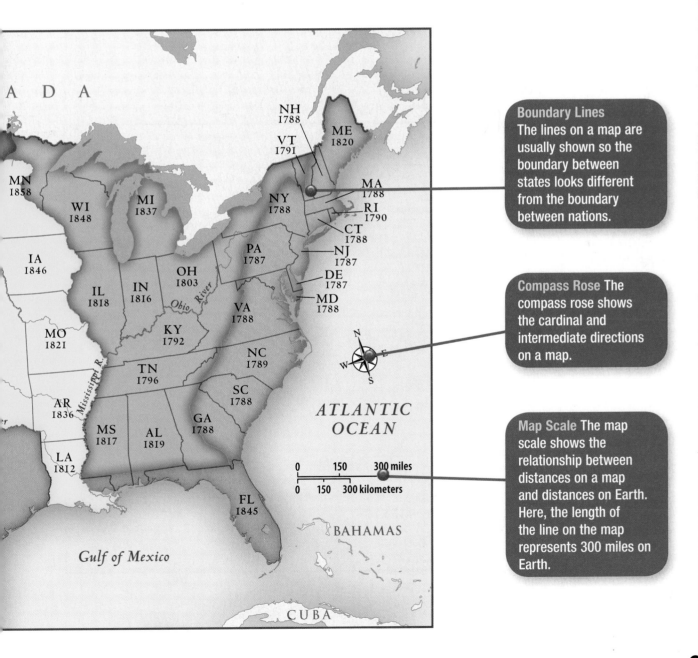

Boundary Lines The lines on a map are usually shown so the boundary between states looks different from the boundary between nations.

Compass Rose The compass rose shows the cardinal and intermediate directions on a map.

Map Scale The map scale shows the relationship between distances on a map and distances on Earth. Here, the length of the line on the map represents 300 miles on Earth.

Use Elevation Maps

An elevation map is a physical map that uses colors to show the elevation, or height of land above or below sea level. The height is usually measured in feet or meters. Sea level is measured as 0 feet or meters around the world. Read the key to understand what each color means. The map on this page uses purple to show land below sea level.

Identify the area of your town or city on the map. How high above sea level is your area?

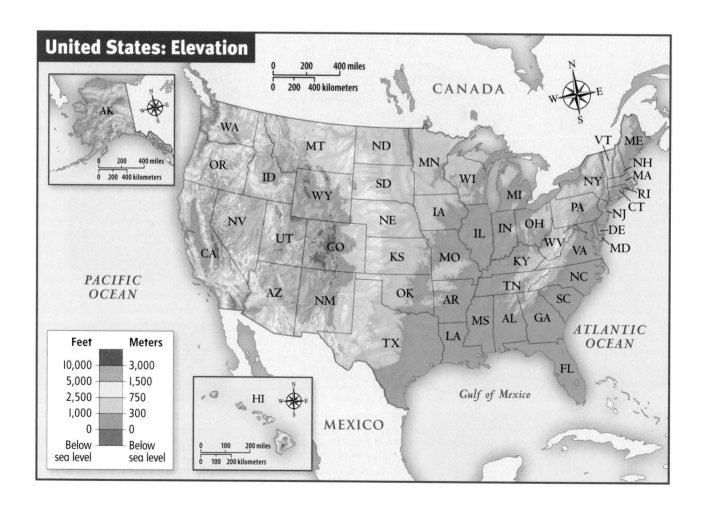

United States: Elevation

Feet	Meters
10,000	3,000
5,000	1,500
2,500	750
1,000	300
0	0
Below sea level	Below sea level

Use Road Maps

Suppose you want to go somewhere you have never been before. How do you know what road to take? You could use a road map. Road maps show where the roads in a certain area go. By reading a road map you can figure out how to get from one place to another.

Look at the road map of Indiana. The map key tells you which kinds of roads are shown on the map. Interstate highways run through two or more states and have two or more lanes in each direction. U.S. highways are usually two lane highways that also connect states. State highways stop at a state's borders. The name of each highway is a number. Notice the different symbols for each of the three kinds of highways.

Which roads would you use to get from South Bend to Terre Haute?

Hemispheres

The equator is an imaginary line on Earth. It divides the sphere of Earth in half. A word for half a sphere is *hemisphere*. The prefix "hemi" means half. Geographers divide Earth into four hemispheres.

All land and ocean north of the equator is in the Northern Hemisphere. All the land and ocean south of the equator is in the Southern Hemisphere.

Another imaginary line on Earth runs from the North Pole to the South Pole. It is called the prime meridian. It divides Earth into the Eastern Hemisphere and the Western Hemisphere.

Is North America in the Northern Hemisphere or Southern Hemisphere?

Is North America in the Eastern Hemisphere or the Western Hemisphere?

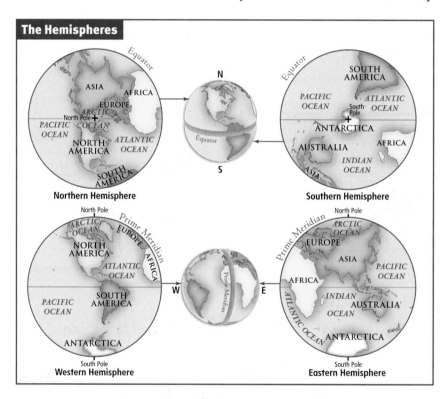

The Hemispheres

Northern Hemisphere

Southern Hemisphere

Western Hemisphere

Eastern Hemisphere

Earth-Sun Relationships

Earth revolves around the sun once a year. As it revolves, Earth also rotates on an axis. An axis is an imaginary line through the center of an object. Earth's axis is tilted 23.5° from due north. That tilt, plus the revolution of Earth around the sun, causes the seasons. The seasons are opposite in the Southern and Northern Hemispheres. For example, when it is winter in the Northern Hemisphere, it is summer in the Southern Hemisphere.

Latitude and Longitude

Geographers have created an imaginary system of lines on the Earth. These lines form a grid to help locate places on any part of the globe. Lines of latitude go from east to west. Lines of longitude go from north to south.

Lines of latitude are called parallels because they are an equal distance apart. The lines of latitude are numbered from 0 at the equator to 90 degrees (°) North at the North Pole and 90° South at the South Pole. Latitude lines usually have N or S to indicate the Northern or Southern Hemisphere.

Lines of longitude, or meridians, circle the Earth from pole to pole. These lines measure the distance from the Prime Meridian, at 0° longitude. Lines of longitude are not parallel. They usually have an E or a W next to the number to indicate the Eastern or Western Hemisphere.

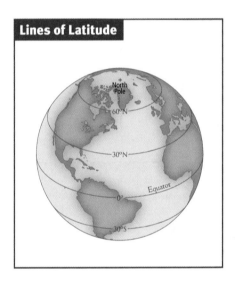

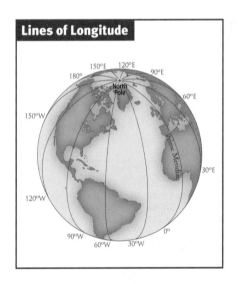

Absolute and Relative Location

You can locate any place on Earth using lines of latitude and longitude. Each line is identified by degrees (°). Each location has a unique number where one line of latitude intersects, or crosses, a line of longitude. This is called its absolute location. Each spot on Earth has an absolute location.

Relative location is the location of a place in relation to other landmarks. For example, St. Louis, Missouri, is located in eastern Missouri, along the Mississippi River.

> **What is your absolute location? Use a map of the United States to find the latitude and longitude of the city or town where you live.**

Maps at Different Scales

All maps are smaller than the real area that they show. To figure out the real distance between two places, most maps include a scale. The scale shows the relationship between distances on a map and real distances.

The scales on the maps in this book are drawn with two horizontal lines. The top line shows distances in miles. The bottom line shows distances in kilometers. You can use a ruler or mark a strip of paper under the scale to measure the distance between places on the map.

The maps on this page are drawn at different scales. Map A and Map B both show the Hawaiian Islands, but Map B shows a larger area with less detail. It is a small-scale map. Map A is a large-scale map. It shows a smaller area with more detail. The scales are different, but the distance between the places shown on both maps is the same.

On both maps, what is the distance in miles between Niihau and Molokai?

What details on Map A are not on Map B?

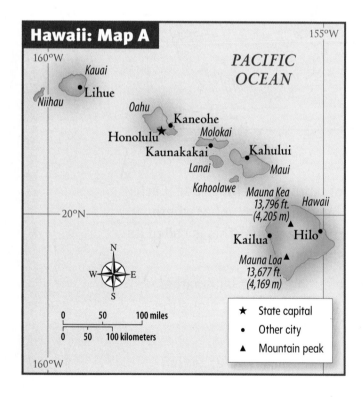

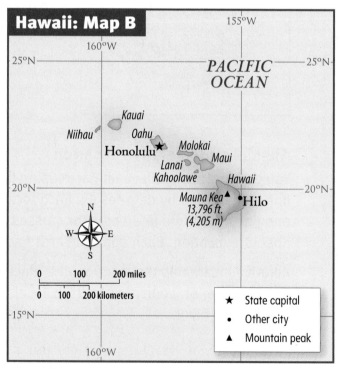

Use Population Maps

When you need to know the number of people who live in a place, or where people live, you can look at a population map. Most population maps show population density—how many people live in a certain area. Another kind of population map shows population distribution—where in an area people live.

Look at the population distribution map of the United States below. Population distribution maps often use different colors to stand for numbers of people per square mile or kilometer. The map key shows the number each color stands for. For example, between 5 and 24 people per square mile live in areas that are shaded yellow.

Which color is used to show the areas with the most people?

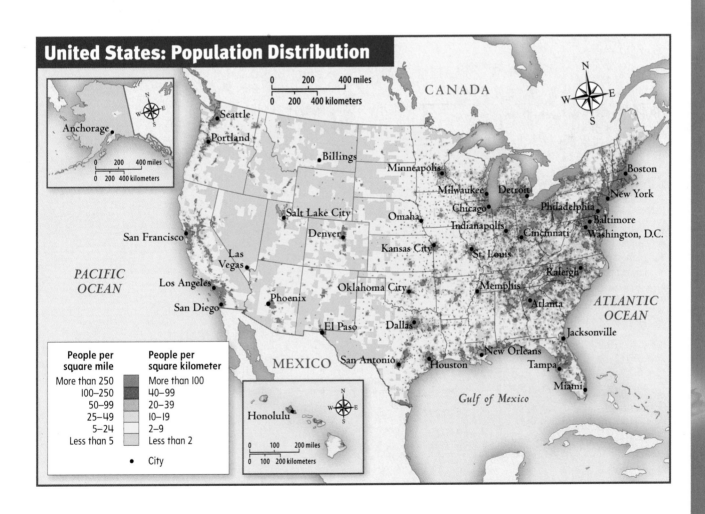

United States: Population Distribution

People per square mile	People per square kilometer
More than 250	More than 100
100–250	40–99
50–99	20–39
25–49	10–19
5–24	2–9
Less than 5	Less than 2
• City	

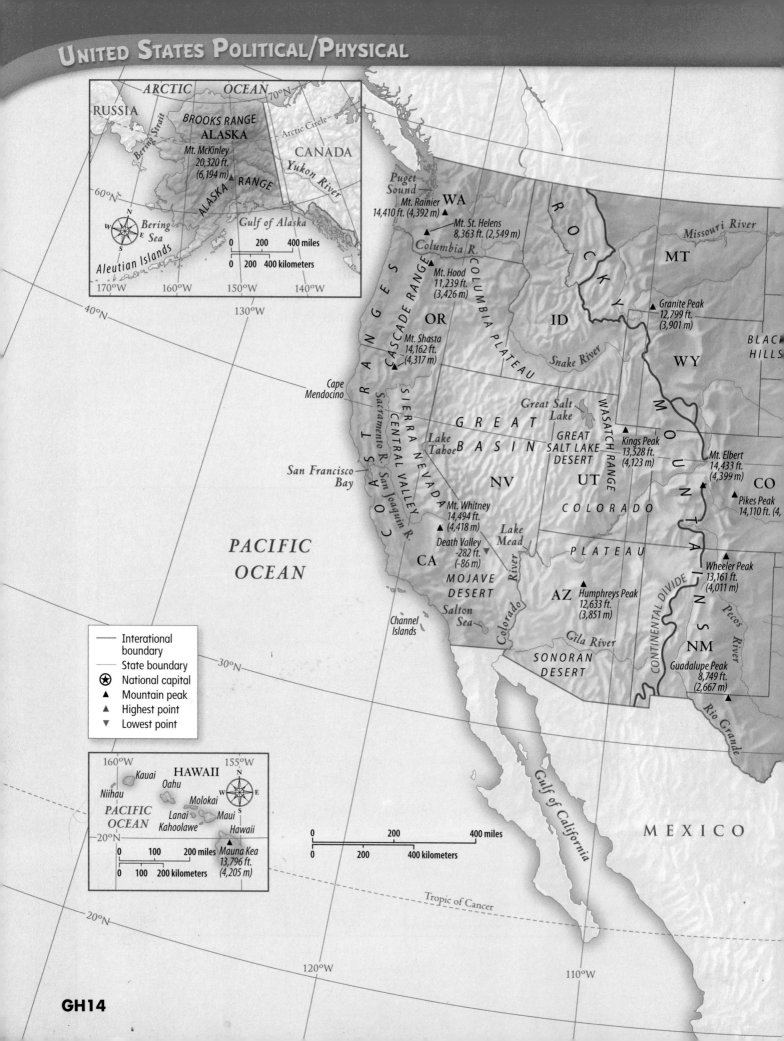

ARCTIC OCEAN
70°N
RUSSIA
BROOKS RANGE
ALASKA
Mt. McKinley
20,320 ft.
(6,194 m)
CANADA
Arctic Circle
Yukon River
Bering Strait
ALASKA RANGE
60°N
N
W E
S
Bering Sea
Gulf of Alaska
Aleutian Islands
0   200   400 miles
0   200   400 kilometers
40°N
170°W   160°W   150°W   140°W
130°W

Puget Sound
Mt. Rainier
14,410 ft. (4,392 m)
WA
Mt. St. Helens
8,363 ft. (2,549 m)
Columbia R.
Mt. Hood
11,239 ft.
(3,426 m)
COLUMBIA PLATEAU
ROCKY
MT
Missouri River
OR
ID
Granite Peak
12,799 ft.
(3,901 m)
Snake River
WY
BLACK HILLS
Mt. Shasta
14,162 ft.
(4,317 m)
Cape Mendocino
Sacramento R.
Central Valley
San Joaquin R.
CASCADE RANGE
COAST RANGES
SIERRA NEVADA
Great Salt Lake
GREAT BASIN
GREAT SALT LAKE DESERT
WASATCH RANGE
Kings Peak
13,528 ft.
(4,123 m)
Mt. Elbert
14,433 ft.
(4,399 m)
CO
Lake Tahoe
NV
UT
COLORADO
Pikes Peak
14,110 ft. (4,
San Francisco Bay
MOUNTAINS
Mt. Whitney
14,494 ft.
(4,418 m)
Lake Mead
CA
Death Valley
-282 ft.
(-86 m)
Colorado River
PLATEAU
Wheeler Peak
13,161 ft.
(4,011 m)
MOJAVE DESERT
AZ
Humphreys Peak
12,633 ft.
(3,851 m)
CONTINENTAL DIVIDE
Pecos River
Salton Sea
Gila River
NM
Channel Islands
SONORAN DESERT
Guadalupe Peak
8,749 ft.
(2,667 m)

PACIFIC OCEAN

30°N

Legend:
— International boundary
— State boundary
⊛ National capital
▲ Mountain peak
▲ Highest point
▼ Lowest point

Rio Grande

Gulf of California

MEXICO

160°W   HAWAII   155°W
Kauai
Oahu
Niihau
PACIFIC OCEAN
Molokai
Lanai   Maui
Kahoolawe
Hawaii
20°N
Mauna Kea
13,796 ft.
(4,205 m)
N
W E
S
0   100   200 miles
0   100   200 kilometers

0   200   400 miles
0   200   400 kilometers

MEXICO

Tropic of Cancer

20°N

120°W   110°W

CANADA

Lake of
the Woods

MESABI
RANGE

Lake Superior

GREAT LAKES

St. Lawrence River

ME

ND

MN

Mississippi River

WI

Lake
Michigan

Lake
Huron

MI

Lake
Ontario

ADIRONDACK
MOUNTAINS

NY

GREEN
MOUNTAINS

VT

Mt. Washington
6,288 ft.
(1,917 m)
▲

NH

MA

Cape Cod

G
R
E
A
T

SD

NE

Platte River

Missouri River

IA

CENTRAL PLAINS

IL

River

OH

ALLEGHENY
PLATEAU

ALLEGHENY
MOUNTAINS

PA

Susquehanna
River

A
P
P
A
L
A
C
H
I
A
N

M
O
U
N
T
A
I
N
S

Hudson River

NJ

CT RI

Long Island

MD DE

Delaware Bay

Washington, D.C.
⍟

KS

IN

Wabash River

Ohio River

WV

Potomac
River

VA

Chesapeake Bay

P
L
A
I
N
S

MO

INTERIOR PLAINS

Arkansas River

OZARK
PLATEAU

KY

TN

Tennessee River

▲ Mt. Mitchell
6,684 ft.
(2,037 m)

PIEDMONT

NC

Cape Hatteras

OK

OUACHITA
MOUNTAINS

AR

Mississippi River

SC

Savannah River

A
T
L
A
N
T
I
C

C
O
A
S
T
A
L

P
L
A
I
N

ATLANTIC
OCEAN

Red River

TX

Brazos River

Colorado River

MS

Alabama River

AL

Chattahoochee River

GA

EDWARDS
PLATEAU

LA

GULF COASTAL PLAIN

Mobile
Bay

FL

Lake
Okeechobee

Galveston
Bay

Mississippi
River Delta

Gulf of Mexico

BAHAMAS

Florida Keys

Straits of Florida

CUBA

N
W   E
S

50°N

40°N

30°N

20°N

100°W

90°W

80°W

GH15

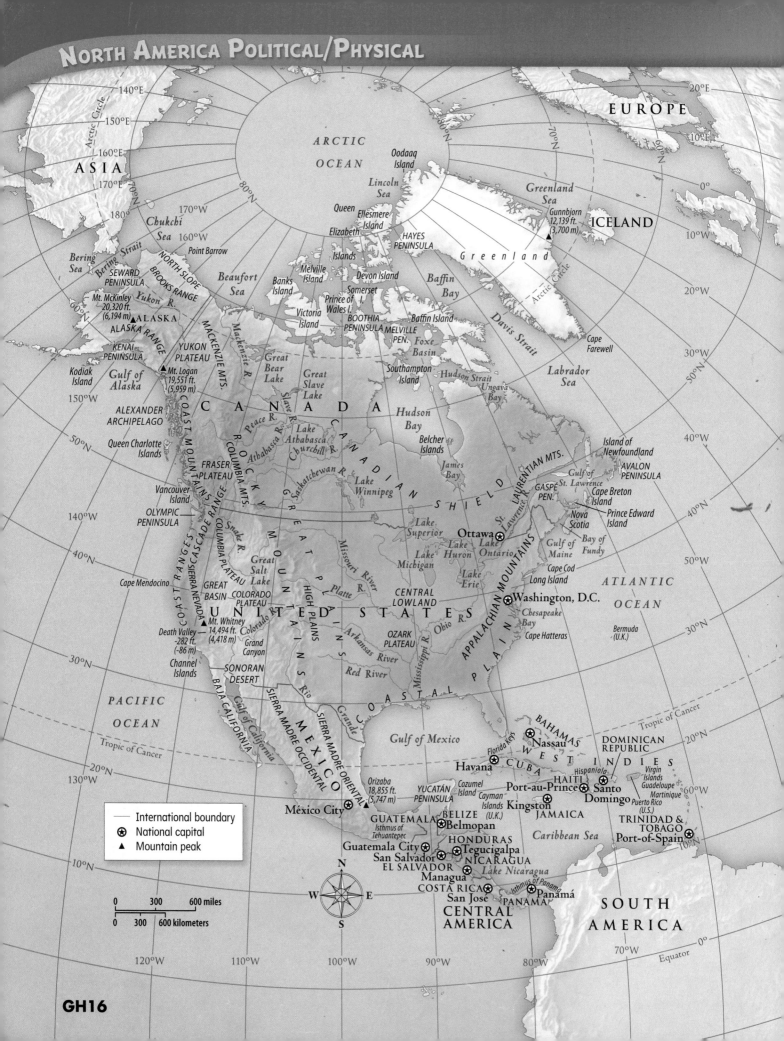

EUROPE

ASIA

ARCTIC OCEAN

20°E
10°E
0°
140°E
150°E
160°E
170°E
180°
170°W
160°W
80°N
70°N

Chukchi Sea

Bering Strait
Bering Sea
NORTH SLOPE
Point Barrow
BROOKS RANGE
SEWARD PENINSULA
Mt. McKinley 20,320 ft. (6,194 m)
ALASKA
ALASKA RANGE
Yukon R.
KENAI PENINSULA
Kodiak Island
Gulf of Alaska
Mt. Logan 19,551 ft. (5,959 m)
MACKENZIE MTS.
YUKON PLATEAU
ALEXANDER ARCHIPELAGO
Queen Charlotte Islands

Beaufort Sea
Banks Island
Melville Island
Victoria Island
Prince of Wales I.
BOOTHIA PENINSULA
Somerset
MELVILLE PEN.
Devon Island
Queen Elizabeth Islands
Ellesmere Island

Lincoln Sea
Oodaaq Island
HAYES PENINSULA

Greenland Sea
Gunnbjorn 12,139 ft. (3,700 m)
ICELAND

Greenland

Baffin Bay
Baffin Island
Foxe Basin
Southampton Island
Hudson Strait
Ungava Bay
Davis Strait
Cape Farewell
Labrador Sea

C A N A D A

Mackenzie R.
Great Bear Lake
Great Slave Lake
Slave R.
Peace R.
Athabasca R.
Lake Athabasca
Saskatchewan R.
Churchill R.
Lake Winnipeg

Hudson Bay
James Bay
Belcher Islands

CANADIAN SHIELD

ROCKY MOUNTAINS
COLUMBIA MTS.
FRASER PLATEAU
Columbia R.
COAST MOUNTAINS
Vancouver Island
OLYMPIC PENINSULA
Fraser R.
CASCADE RANGE
COLUMBIA PLATEAU
Snake R.
GREAT BASIN
Great Salt Lake
SIERRA NEVADA
COAST RANGES
Cape Mendocino
COLORADO PLATEAU
Mt. Whitney 14,494 ft. (4,418 m)
Death Valley -282 ft. (-86 m)
Grand Canyon
Channel Islands
Colorado R.
HIGH PLAINS
Platte R.
Missouri River
G R E A T   P L A I N S

Lake Superior
Lake Michigan
Lake Huron
Lake Erie
Lake Ontario
Ottawa

LAURENTIAN MTS.
St. Lawrence R.
GASPÉ PEN.
Gulf of St. Lawrence
Island of Newfoundland
AVALON PENINSULA
Cape Breton Island
Nova Scotia
Prince Edward Island
Bay of Fundy
Gulf of Maine
Cape Cod
Long Island

U N I T E D   S T A T E S

CENTRAL LOWLAND
Arkansas River
OZARK PLATEAU
Ohio R.
Mississippi R.
Red River
APPALACHIAN MOUNTAINS
Washington, D.C.
Chesapeake Bay
Cape Hatteras
C O A S T A L   P L A I N
Bermuda (U.K.)

ATLANTIC OCEAN

SONORAN DESERT
BAJA CALIFORNIA
Gulf of California
M E X I C O
Rio Grande
SIERRA MADRE OCCIDENTAL
SIERRA MADRE ORIENTAL
Orizaba 18,855 ft. (5,747 m)
México City
YUCATÁN PENINSULA
Cozumel Island

PACIFIC OCEAN

Gulf of Mexico
Florida Keys
BAHAMAS
Nassau
Havana
CUBA
W E S T   I N D I E S
Cayman Islands (U.K.)
Kingston
JAMAICA
Caribbean Sea
HAITI
Port-au-Prince
Hispaniola
DOMINICAN REPUBLIC
Santo Domingo
Puerto Rico (U.S.)
Virgin Islands
Guadeloupe
Martinique
TRINIDAD & TOBAGO
Port-of-Spain

Tropic of Cancer

GUATEMALA
BELIZE
Belmopan
Guatemala City
Isthmus of Tehuantepec
HONDURAS
Tegucigalpa
San Salvador
EL SALVADOR
NICARAGUA
Managua
Lake Nicaragua
COSTA RICA
San José
Isthmus of Panama
PANAMA
Panamá

CENTRAL AMERICA

SOUTH AMERICA

Equator

—	International boundary
✪	National capital
▲	Mountain peak

0   300   600 miles
0   300   600 kilometers

N
W   E
S

70°N
60°N
50°N
40°N
30°N
20°N
10°N

140°W
130°W
120°W
110°W
100°W
90°W
80°W
70°W

20°W
30°W
40°W
50°W
60°W

SOUTH AMERICA POLITICAL/PHYSICAL

NORTH AMERICA

ISTHMUS OF PANAMA

Caribbean Sea

15°N

Maracaibo

⊛ Caracas

Orinoco R.

VENEZUELA

GUIANA HIGHLANDS

⊛ Bogotá

GUYANA

⊛ Georgetown

• Paramaribo

SURINAME

• Cayenne

FRENCH GUIANA (France)

Cali •

COLOMBIA

Quito ⊛

ECUADOR

Guayaquil •

Negro River

ATLANTIC OCEAN

Equator 0°

Amazon River

River

Tapajos River

Xingú River

Tocantins River

São Francisco River

Galápagos Islands (Ecuador)

AMAZON BASIN

PERU

Madeira River

BRAZIL

Lima ⊛

Arequipa •

Lake Titicaca

⊛ La Paz

BOLIVIA

Sucre ⊛

• Santa Cruz

BRAZILIAN

Brasília ⊛

HIGHLANDS

15°S

River

ATACAMA DESERT

Mt. Ojos del Salado 22,572 ft. (6,880 m) ▲

Paraguay R.

PARAGUAY

Paraná

Rio de Janeiro •

São Paulo •

Tropic of Capricorn

CHILE

Mt. Aconcagua 22,834 ft. (6,960 m) ▲

Asunción ⊛

Paraná River

Tropic of Capricorn

ANDES MOUNTAINS

Rosario •

Valparaíso ⊛
Santiago

ARGENTINA

URUGUAY

• Salto

Montevideo ⊛

Rio de la Plata

PACIFIC OCEAN

Concepción •

Buenos Aires ⊛

PAMPAS

30°S

P A T A G O N I A

ATLANTIC OCEAN

45°S

Falkland Islands (Islas Malvinas) (U.K.)

| 0 | 250 | 500 miles |
| 0 | 250 | 500 kilometers |

Strait of Magellan

TIERRA DEL FUEGO

South Georgia (U.K.)

Cape Horn

Legend
— International boundary
⊛ National capital
• Other city
▲ Mountain peak

105°W 90°W 75°W 60°W 45°W 30°W

GH17

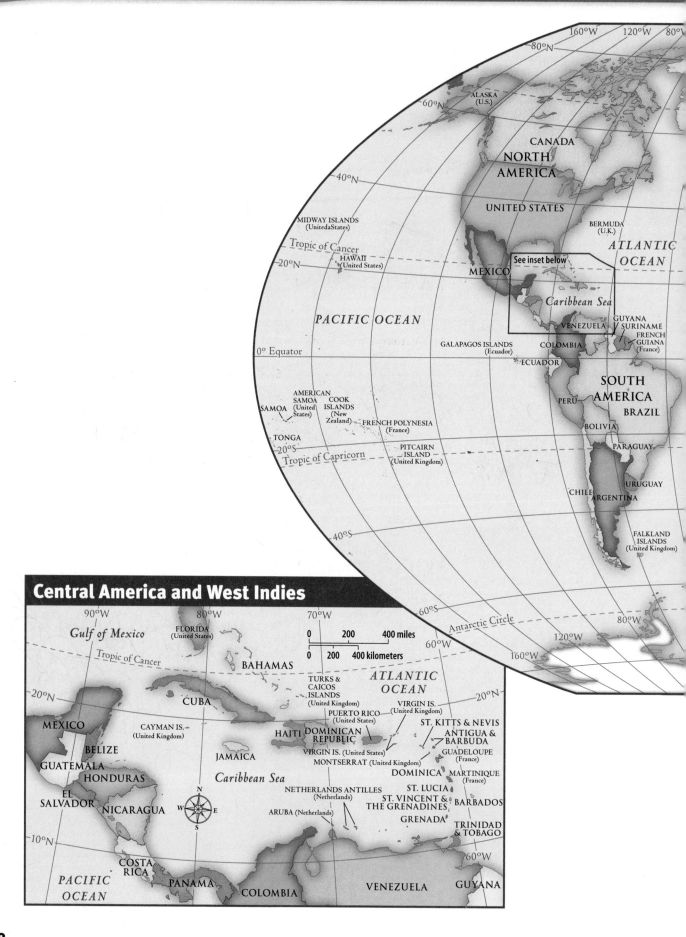

ALASKA
(U.S.)

CANADA

NORTH AMERICA

UNITED STATES

BERMUDA
(U.K.)

MIDWAY ISLANDS
(UnitedaStates)

Tropic of Cancer

HAWAII
(United States)

MEXICO

Caribbean Sea

ATLANTIC OCEAN

See inset below

GUYANA
SURINAME
FRENCH
GUIANA
(France)

VENEZUELA

GALAPAGOS ISLANDS
(Ecuador)

COLOMBIA

ECUADOR

PACIFIC OCEAN

0° Equator

SOUTH AMERICA

PERU

BRAZIL

AMERICAN
SAMOA
(United
States)

COOK
ISLANDS
(New
Zealand)

SAMOA

FRENCH POLYNESIA
(France)

BOLIVIA

TONGA

PARAGUAY

PITCAIRN
ISLAND
(United Kingdom)

Tropic of Capricorn

CHILE

URUGUAY

ARGENTINA

FALKLAND
ISLANDS
(United Kingdom)

Antarctic Circle

Central America and West Indies

Gulf of Mexico

FLORIDA
(United States)

Tropic of Cancer

BAHAMAS

ATLANTIC OCEAN

0   200   400 miles

0   200   400 kilometers

TURKS &
CAICOS
ISLANDS
(United Kingdom)

VIRGIN IS.
(United Kingdom)

CUBA

PUERTO RICO
(United States)

ST. KITTS & NEVIS

MEXICO

CAYMAN IS.
(United Kingdom)

HAITI

DOMINICAN
REPUBLIC

ANTIGUA &
BARBUDA

BELIZE

JAMAICA

VIRGIN IS. (United States)

GUADELOUPE
(France)

GUATEMALA

MONTSERRAT (United Kingdom)

HONDURAS

Caribbean Sea

DOMINICA

MARTINIQUE
(France)

EL
SALVADOR

NICARAGUA

N
W   E
S

NETHERLANDS ANTILLES
(Netherlands)

ST. LUCIA

ST. VINCENT &
THE GRENADINES

BARBADOS

ARUBA (Netherlands)

GRENADA

TRINIDAD
& TOBAGO

COSTA
RICA

PACIFIC
OCEAN

PANAMA

COLOMBIA

VENEZUELA

GUYANA

ARCTIC OCEAN

40°W 0° 40°E 80°E 120°E 160°E
80°N

GREENLAND
(Denmark)

SVALBARD
(Norway)

Arctic Circle

ICELAND

See inset below

RUSSIA

60°N

EUROPE

ASIA

40°N

KAZAKHSTAN MONGOLIA

AZORES
(Portugal)

GEORGIA UZBEKISTAN KYRGYZSTAN

NORTH
KOREA

JAPAN

PACIFIC
OCEAN

ARMENIA TURKMENISTAN TAJIKISTAN SOUTH
KOREA

TURKEY

TUNISIA LEBANON SYRIA AZERBAIJAN AFGHANISTAN CHINA

CANARY
ISLANDS
(Spain)

MOROCCO

IRAQ IRAN PAKISTAN

ISRAEL KUWAIT BHUTAN

Tropic of Cancer

WESTERN
SAHARA
(Morocco)

ALGERIA LIBYA EGYPT

JORDAN BAHRAIN NEPAL

QATAR BANGLADESH TAIWAN

20°N

WAKE
ISLAND
(United States)

SAUDI
ARABIA

UNITED
ARAB
EMIRATES

INDIA

MYANMAR
(BURMA)

NORTHERN
MARIANA
ISLANDS
(United States)

GUAM
(United States)

MARSHALL
ISLANDS

CAPE
VERDE

MAURITANIA

MALI NIGER

ERITREA

YEMEN OMAN

LAOS

THAILAND VIETNAM

SENEGAL
GAMBIA
GUINEA-
BISSAU GUINEA

CHAD SUDAN

DJIBOUTI

PHILIPPINES

FEDERATED STATES
OF MICRONESIA

PALAU

KIRIBATI

BURKINA
FASO

AFRICA

SRI
LANKA

CAMBODIA
BRUNEI

SIERRA LEONE GHANA
LIBERIA

NIGERIA CENTRAL
AFRICAN
REPUBLIC

BENIN

ETHIOPIA

SOMALIA

MALAYSIA

Equator 0°

NAURU

COTE D'IVOIRE TOGO
SAO TOME AND PRINCIPE

CAMEROON

UGANDA KENYA

MALDIVES

EQUATORIAL GUINEA GABON
CONGO

RWANDA
DEM.
REPUBLIC
OF THE
CONGO BURUNDI

TANZANIA

SEYCHELLES

INDONESIA

EAST
TIMOR

PAPUA
NEW
GUINEA

SOLOMON
ISLANDS

ATLANTIC
OCEAN

COMOROS

TUVALU

ANGOLA

ZAMBIA MALAWI

INDIAN
OCEAN

NAMIBIA ZIMBABWE MADAGASCAR

BOTSWANA

MAURITIUS

Tropic of Capricorn

VANUATU FIJI
ISLANDS

20°S

MOZAMBIQUE REUNION
(France)

SWAZILAND

NEW
CALEDONIA
(France)

SOUTH
AFRICA LESOTHO

AUSTRALIA

N

W E

S

SOUTH GEORGIA &
SOUTH SANDWICH
ISLANDS (United Kingdom)

FRENCH SOUTHERN &
ANTARCTIC LANDS
(France)

0 1,000 2,000 miles

40°S

NEW
ZEALAND

0 1,000 2,000 kilometers

40°E 80°E 120°E 160°E 60°S

Antarctic Circle

40°W 0° ANTARCTICA

80°S

Europe

20°E 30°E 40°E 50°E

NORWAY FINLAND RUSSIA

60°N SWEDEN

North
Sea

ESTONIA

0 200 400 miles

0 200 400 kilometers

Baltic Sea LATVIA

N

IRELAND UNITED
KINGDOM

DENMARK LITHUANIA W E

RUSSIA S

NETHERLANDS

BELARUS

ATLANTIC
OCEAN

BELGIUM GERMANY POLAND

LUXEMBOURG CZECH
REPUBLIC

UKRAINE

50°N

LIECHTENSTEIN

FRANCE SLOVAKIA

SWITZERLAND AUSTRIA HUNGARY MOLDOVA

RUSSIA

SLOVENIA ROMANIA

MONACO CROATIA

Black Sea GEORGIA

40°N ANDORRA SAN
MARINO BOSNIA &
HERZEGOVINA

SERBIA

PORTUGAL SPAIN CORSICA
(France)

MONT.
MACEDONIA

BULGARIA

40°N

ITALY ALBANIA TURKEY

SARDINIA
(Italy)

BALEARIC IS.
(Spain)

SICILY
(Italy)

GREECE

GIBRALTAR (U.K.) 10°E

MALTA CRETE (Gr.) CYPRUS SYRIA

MOROCCO 0° ALGERIA TUNISIA 20°E Mediterranean Sea 30°E LEBANON

ARCTIC OCEAN

160°W   120°W   80°W   40°W

80°N

GREENLAND

Mackenzie River

60°N   ALASKA RANGE

Arctic Circle

Mt. McKinley
20,320 ft.
(6,194 m)

ROCKY MOUNTAINS

CANADIAN SHIELD

NORTH
AMERICA

40°N

Mississippi River

APPALACHIAN MTS.

PACIFIC OCEAN

ATLANTIC
OCEAN

Tropic of Cancer

Rio Grande

20°N

Gulf of
Mexico

Caribbean Sea

0°   Equator

Amazon River

SOUTH
AMERICA

ANDES

20°S   Tropic of Capricorn

Mt. Aconcagua
22,834 ft.
(6,960 m)

MOUNTAINS

ATLANTIC
OCEAN

40°S

PACIFIC OCEAN

Cape Horn

60°S

80°W

Weddell
Sea

Antarctic Circle

120°W

40°W

160°W

Vinson Massif ▲
16,067 ft.
(4,897 m)

ARCTIC OCEAN

40°E   80°E   120°E   160°E   80°N

Lena
River

Yenisey River

Ob River   60°N

URAL MTS.

Volga River

Sea of Okhotsk

EUROPE

Caspian Sea

ASIA   GOBI   40°N

ALPS

Mont Blanc
15,711 ft.
(4,807 m)   Black Sea   Mt. Elbrus
18,510 ft.
(5,642 m)   HINDU KUSH

Mediterranean Sea

SYRIAN
DESERT   HIMALAYA   Yangtze River

Tropic of Cancer

SAHARA   Ganges River   Mt. Everest
29,035 ft.
(8,850 m)   20°N

Red Sea   DECCAN
PLATEAU

Nile River   Arabian
Sea   South
China
Sea   Philippine
Sea   PACIFIC OCEAN

AFRICA

Congo River   Mt. Kilimanjaro
19,340 ft.
(5,895 m)   Equator   0°

INDIAN
OCEAN

Coral
Sea

NAMIB DESERT   KALAHARI
DESERT   Tropic of Capricorn   GREAT
SANDY
DESERT   20°S

AUSTRALIA   Darling River

Cape of
Good Hope   Mt. Kosciuszko
7,310 ft.
(2,228 m)

N
W   E
S   40°S

0   1,000   2,000 miles
0   1,000   2,000 kilometers

40°E   80°E   120°E   Antarctic Circle   160°E   60°S

ANTARCTICA   80°S

Glossary

This Glossary will help you to pronounce and understand the meanings of the vocabulary terms in this book. The page number at the end of the definition tells you where the word first appears.

A

absolute location (ab′sə lüt lō kā′shən) exact location of a place expressed by longitude and latitude or street address (p. 17)

acid rain (a′sid rān) precipitation containing harmful chemical pollution that can destroy trees and wildlife and poison water; see **precipitation** (p. 121)

altitude (al′ti tüd) height of something above the ground or above sea level (p. 154)

amendment (ə mend′mənt) an addition to the Constitution (p. 72)

annex (an′eks) to make a country or territory part of another country (p. 56)

archipelago (är kə pel′ə gō) a cluster of many islands (p. 135)

arid (ar′id) dry (p. 32)

assembly (ə sem′blē) a lawmaking body (p. 64)

B

barrio (bä′ rē ō) city neighborhood in which many Spanish-speaking people live (p. 248)

battle map (bat′əl map) a map that shows the events of a conflict between two groups of armed forces (p. 185)

bilingual (bī ling′wəl) having two languages (p. 87)

biotechnology (bī ō tech nol′ə gē) technology that uses living cells to create new drugs (p. 102)

blizzard (bliz′ərd) heavy snowstorm with very strong winds (p. 37)

C

campesino (käm pə sē′ nō) a poor farmer (p. 221)

canal (kə nal′) a human-built waterway (p. 139)

canyon (kan′yən) deep valley with very high, steep sides (p. 11)

PRONUNCIATION KEY

a	at	ē	me	ō	old	ū	use	ng	song
ā	ape	i	it	ô	fork	ü	rule	th	thin
ä	far	ī	ice	oi	oil	ů	pull	th	this
âr	care	î	pierce	ou	out	ûr	turn	zh	measure
e	end	o	hot	u	up	hw	white	ə	about, taken, pencil, lemon, circus

carnival (kär′nǝ vǝl) a festival held on the last day before the Christian holy period of Lent (p. 203)

cartogram (kär′tǝ gram) a map that shows information by changing the sizes of places (p. 233)

cash crop (kash krop) farm product grown for export (p. 177)

caudillo (kou dē′yō) military dictator of nineteenth-century Latin America (p. 187)

checks and balances (cheks and bal′ǝn sǝz) system that balances power among the branches of government (p. 69)

circle graph (sûr′kǝl graf) chart that shows how something can be divided into parts (p. 125)

climograph (klī′mō graf) graph that shows information about the temperature and precipitation of a place over time (p. 157)

Columbian Exchange (kǝ lum′bē ǝn eks chānj′) the movement of people, plants, animals, and germs in either direction across the Atlantic Ocean following the voyages of Columbus (p. 147)

command economy (kǝ mand′ ē kon′ǝ mē) an economy completely controlled by the government (p. 230)

commonwealth (kom′ǝn welth) the government of a nation or a state; as a United States commonwealth, Puerto Rico has control over its local affairs (p. 230)

communism (kom′ūn izm) system of government in which the government controls the economy, and people have limited rights to own property (p. 192)

conservation (kon sǝr vā′shǝn) protection and careful use of natural resources (p. 121)

Continental Divide (kon′tǝ nen′tǝl di vīd′) imaginary line made of high points in the Rockies from where our nation's rivers flow east or west (p. 7)

current (kûr′ǝnt) a portion of water or air that flows continuously in approximately the same path (p. 28)

D
---

decree (di krē′) a royal command (p. 183)

default (dē folt′) failure to pay a financial debt (p. 243)

deforestation (dē for ǝ stā′shǝn) the process of clearing forests (p. 144)

demand (di mand′) the desire for a product or service; see **supply** (p. 104)

developed nation (dē vel′ǝpt nā′shǝn) a country with a high level of economic development that includes high technology, services, manufacturing, and extraction such as fishing, forestry, and mining (p. 109)

dictator (dik′tā tǝr) a leader with complete power over a country (p. 187)

drought (drout) long period of little or no rainfall (p. 30)

E
---

economic growth (ē kǝ′ nä mik grōth) an economy's increase in the value of goods and services (p. 109)

economy (ē kon′ǝ mē) the way a country's people use natural resources, money, and knowledge to produce goods and services (p. 22)

ecosystem (ē′kō sis tǝm) all the living and nonliving things in a certain area (p. 238)

El Niño (el nē′nyō) weather event marked by very heavy rains in western South America, often causing flooding; reduced rainfall in in Southern Asia, Australia, and Africa; and severe storms in North America; opposite of La Niña (p. 156)

emigrate (e′mə grāt) to leave a country and move to another (p. 196)

empire (em′pīr) an area in which different groups of people are controlled by one ruler or government (p. 170)

encomienda (en kō mē en′də) a Spanish grant of land that included all the Native Americans living on the land (p. 177)

F

favela (fä′ve lə) an overcrowded city slum in Brazil (p. 235)

federalism (fed′ər əl izm) a system of government in which power in the nation is shared between the central government and the state governments (p. 70)

fossil fuel (fos′əl fū′əl) fuel, such as oil, natural gas, and coal, that is formed from the remains of plants and animals that lived millions of years ago (p. 121)

free enterprise (frē en′tər prīz) economic system in which people can own property and businesses and are free to decide what to make, how much to produce, and what price to charge (p. 101)

FTA (Free Trade Agreement) (frē trād a grē′mənt) an agreement signed by Canada and the United States in 1987 that increased trade over a ten year period (p. 115)

G

gasohol (ga sə′hol) human-made fuel produced from mixing gasoline and alcohol made from sugarcane (p. 144)

gaucho (gau′chō) cowhand in Argentina (p. 242)

glacier (glā′shər) a large mass of ice (p. 14)

global grid (glō′bəl grid) a set of squares formed by crisscrossing lines that can help you determine the absolute location of a place on a globe (p. 17)

global warming (glō′bəl wär′ming) the gradual increase of the Earth's temperature (p. 40)

glyph (glif) a picture symbol (p. 166)

gross domestic product (GDP) (grōs də mes′tik prod′əkt) the total value of all the goods produced in a country in one year (p. 247)

H

historical map (his tôr′i kəl map) a map that shows information about the past or where past events took place (p. 67)

hunter-gatherer (hun′tər gath′ər ər) one who hunted animals and gathered wild plants for food (p. 148)

hurricane (hûr′i kän) cyclonic storm with very strong winds and heavy rain (p. 36)

hydroelectric power (hī drô i lek′trik pou′ər) electricity made from flowing water in rivers (p. 20)

I

indigenous (in di′jə nəs) people descended from an area's first inhabitants (p. 53)

interdependence (in'tər di pen'dəns) dependence on each other to meet needs and wants (p. 115)

irrigation (ir i gā'shən) a method of supplying dry land with water though a series of ditches or pipes (p. 25)

isthmus (is'məs) a narrow stretch of land with water on both sides (p. 139)

J
---

jade (jād) shiny stone that comes in many shades of green (p. 165)

junta (jən'tə or hun'tə) a group of people controlling a government (p. 226)

K
---

knowledge economy (nä'lij i kä'nə mē) an economy that makes a profit on the production and management of information; biotechnology is an industry in a knowledge economy (p. 111)

L

La Niña (lä nē'nyə) weather event marked by unusually cool waters in the eastern Pacific and low amounts of rainfall there and heavier rains–and a better chance of hurricanes–in the western Pacific; opposite of El Niño (p. 156)

large-scale map (lärj skāl map) map that shows a smaller area in greater detail; see **small-scale map** (p. 119)

latitude (lat'i tüd) imaginary line, or parallel, measuring distance north or south of the equator; see **parallel** (p. 17)

levee (le vē) an earth wall that farmers built to keep water from overflowing onto the land (p. 44)

line graph (līn graf) graph that shows changes over time (p. 125)

Line of Demarcation (līn əv di mär kā'shən) an agreed-upon imaginary line dividing the Americas into Spanish and Portuguese territories in 1494 (p. 173)

literacy rate (li'tə rə sē rāt) percentage of people who can read and write (p. 224)

Llanos ('lä'nōs) tropical grasslands that stretch through eastern Colombia and Venezuela (p. 136)

PRONUNCIATION KEY

a	at	ē	me	ō	old	ū	use	ng	song
ā	ape	i	it	ô	fork	ü	rule	th	thin
ä	far	ī	ice	oi	oil	u̇	pull	th	this
âr	care	î	pierce	ou	out	ûr	turn	zh	measure
e	end	o	hot	u	up	hw	white	ə	about, taken, pencil, lemon, circus

longitude (lon′ji tüd) imaginary line, or meridian, measuring distance east or west of the prime meridian; see **meridian** and **prime meridian** (p. 17)

Loyalist (loi′ə list) a colonist who supported Great Britain in the American Revolution (p. 64)

M

map scale (map skāl) a line like a measuring stick drawn on a map that uses a unit of measurement, such as an inch, to represent a real distance on Earth (p. 119)

maquiladora (mə′kē lə dor ə) foreign-owned factory in Mexico where workers assemble parts made in other countries (p. 216)

megalopolis (meg ə lop′ə lis) large urban area formed by several cities (p. 6)

meridian (mə rid′ē ən) any line of longitude east or west of Earth's prime meridian; see **longitude** and **prime meridian** (p. 17)

mestizo (mãs tē′zō) a person of mixed Spanish and Native American heritage (p. 180)

migrant worker (mī′grənt wûr′kər) a laborer who moves from place to place to find work (p. 219)

migrate (mī′grāt) to move from one place to another (p. 196)

monarch (mon′ärk) the head of government based on the rule of a king or queen (p. 75)

mulatto (mə lat′ō) a person of mixed African and European ancestry (p. 198)

multiculturalism (mul tē kul′chər əl izm) adapting to diverse cultures (p. 87)

mural (myur′əl) large paintings painted on a wall (p. 204)

N

national debt (na′shən nəl det) the amount of money a country owes to other countries (p. 243)

navigable (na′vi gə bəl) waterway that is deep enough and wide enough for ships to steer through (p. 13)

Northwest Passage (nôrth′west pas′ij) water route believed to flow through North America to Asia that European explorers searched for from the 1500s to the 1700s (p. 62)

O

obsidian (ob si′ dē ən) glassy rock formed from the lava of volcanoes (p. 165)

P

Pampas (pam′pəz) treeless grassland of Argentina and Uruguay (p. 136)

parallel (par′ə lel) line of latitude; see **latitude** (p. 17)

parallel time line (par′ə lel tīm′līn) two different sets of events on the same time line (p. 73)

parliament (pär′lə mənt) an assembly of people who pass laws and govern a nation (p. 75)

pidgin language (pij′ən lang′gwij) language formed by combining several different languages (p. 199)

plantation (plan tā′shən) a large farm that often grows one cash crop (p. 177)

plate tectonics (plăt tek ton'iks) theory that Earth's surface is made up of plates that are constantly moving (p. 38)

plaza (plä'zə) public square in a Latin American city around which government buildings and major churches were built (p. 213)

prairie (prâr'ē) flat or rolling land covered with grass (p. 8)

precipitation (pri sip i tā'shən) moisture that falls to the ground in the form of rain, sleet, hail, or snow (p. 28)

prime meridian (prīm mə rid'ē ən) line of longitude labeled 0° longitude; any place east of the prime meridian is labeled E; any place west of it is labeled W; see **longitude** (p. 17)

prime minister (prīm min'ə stər) head of a parliamentary government (p. 75)

profit (prof'it) money a business earns after it pays for tools, salaries, and other costs (p. 101)

province (prov'ins) a political division of a country (p. 65)

R
---

rain forest (rān for əst) a dense area of trees and plants that receives a lot of rain (p. 144)

relative location (rel'ə tiv lō kā'shən) the location of a place in relation to another place (p. 17)

renewable resource (ri nü'ə bəl rē'sôrs) material found in nature that can be replaced, such as forests (p. 20)

representative democracy (rep'ri zen'tə tiv di mok'rə sē) form of government in which voters choose leaders who make and enforce laws (p. 69)

rural (rür'əl) of the countryside (p. 84)

S
---

scarcity (skâr'si tē) shortage of available goods and services (p. 22)

selva (sel'və) Brazilian name for the Amazonian rain forest (p. 238)

separatism (sep'ər ə ti zim) a belief in separating from a nation (p. 88)

slavery (slā'və rē) the practice of people's owning other people and forcing them to work (p. 56)

small-scale map (smôl skāl map) map that shows a large area but not much detail; see **large-scale map** (p. 119)

smog (smog) thick haze of smoke and chemicals (p. 218)

PRONUNCIATION KEY

a	at	ē	me	ō	old	ū	use	ng	song
ā	ape	i	it	ô	fork	ü	rule	th	thin
ä	far	ī	ice	oi	oil	ů	pull	th	this
âr	care	î	pierce	ou	out	ûr	turn	zh	measure
e	end	o	hot	u	up	hw	white	ə	about, taken, pencil, lemon, circus

socialism (sō'shə liz'əm) economic system under which all land, banks, factories, and large businesses are owned and controlled by the government, not by individuals (p. 193)

stock (stok) a share in the ownership of a company (p. 101)

subregion (sub rē'jen) smaller area of a region (p. 133)

subsistence farm (səb sis'təns färm) small plot of land on which a farmer grows only enough food to feed his or her family (p. 217)

suburb (sə'bûrb) community near a city (p. 84)

supply (sə plī') quantity of something needed or ready for use; see **demand** (p. 104)

T
---

tariff (tar'if) tax added to the price of goods that are imported (p. 115)

temperate climate (tem'pər it klī'mit) mild weather that is neither too hot nor too cold, with changing seasons (p. 27)

territory (ter'i tôr ē) an area of land controlled by a nation (p. 65)

terrorism (ter'ər izm) the use of fear and violence to gain political goals (p. 59)

time line (tīm' līn) a diagram showing the order in which events took place (p. 73)

time zone (tīm zōn) one of the 24 areas into which Earth is divided for measuring time (p. 137)

tornado (tôr nā'dō) powerful windstorm with a funnel-shaped cloud that moves quickly over land (p. 35)

trade deficit (trād def'ə sit) situation that occurs when the value of a country's imports is higher than the value of its exports (p. 116)

trade surplus (trād sûr'plus) situation that occurs when the value of a country's exports is higher than the value of its imports (p. 116)

treaty (trē'tē) agreement to make peace (p. 56)

tributary (trib'yə ter ē) river or stream that flows into a larger river (p. 13)

tundra (tun'drə) treeless plain where only grasses and mosses can grow (p. 5)

U
---

urban (ûr'bən) of the city (p. 84)

urbanization (ûr bə nə zā'shən) population movement from rural areas to cities (p. 124)

urban sprawl (ûr'bən sprôl) spread of human settlements into natural areas (p. 124)

V
---

vaquero (vä kâr'ō) Mexican cowhand (p. 216)

voyageur (vwä yä zhûr') trader who transported furs by canoe in New France (p. 62)

W
---

water table (wô'tər tā bəl) underground water that is close to land surface (p. 45)

wetland (wet'land) low, flat area covered with water (p. 16)

Index

This index lists many topics that appear in the book, along with the pages on which they are found. Page numbers after a *c* refer you to a chart, after a *d* refer you to a diagram, after a *g* refer you to a graph, after an *m* refer you to a map, after a *p* refer you to photographs, after a *q* refer you to a quote.

Index

Credits

Getty Images. 199: (tr) Patrick Robert/Sygma/CORBIS; (bcl) Jean-Yves Rabeuf-Valette / The Image Works; (tl) Hans Neleman/Getty Images. 201: Kevin Schafer/CORBIS. 202: (cr) Associated Press; (t) Associated Press. 203; (tcl) Scott B. Rosen ; (inset) Associated Press. 204: (br) LAURA BOUSHNAK/AFP/Getty Images; (tr) Albright-Knox Art Gallery/CORBIS; (tl) Diego Giudice/Corbis; (bl) Rufus F. Folkks/Corbis. 204-205 (bkgd) Scott B. Rosen. 205: (b) Hulton Archive/Getty Images; (tr) Archivo Iconografico, S.A./CORBIS; (tr) Associated Press. 206-207 (bkgd) Laura Siciliano-Rosen. 209: Organization of American States.212: (tl) AFP/Getty Images; (tr) Time Life Pictures/Time Magazine, Copyright Time Inc./Time Life Pictures/Getty Images; (br) Stephanie Maze/CORBIS; (bkgd) Stephanie Maze/CORBIS; 212 (bl) Brand X Pictures/PunchStock. 213: (b) Chris Sharp; (tl) Reuters/CORBIS; (bl) Alfredo Maiquez; (tr) TIMOTHY A. CLARY/AFP/Getty Images. 214: (b) Randy Faris/CORBIS; (t) Associated Press. 215: (t) Scott B. Rosen; (c) Scott B. Rosen; (b) Scott B. Rosen. 216: Associated Press. 217: Jeff Greenberg / PhotoEdit . 220: Martin Rogers/CORBIS. 222: Eliana Aponte. REUTERS. 223: (bcr) Photodisc/PunchStock; (c) Eric Vernazobres/Corbis. 224: (bcl) G.RACINAN/WITNESS/CORBIS SYGMA. 225: (bc) John Davenport/Getty Images; 226: (t) Thomas Shjarback / Alamy. 227: (bcl) AFP/Getty Images; (b) AFP/Getty Images. 228: Bill Gentile/CORBIS. 229: Photographer's Choice/PunchStock. 230: (inset) Reuters/CORBIS; (t) Rachel Royse/CORBIS; (l) David R. Frazier / Danita Delimont Agency / drr.net. 231: (t) Domond, Wilmino (b.1925) / Private Collection, Photo © Held Collection / The Bridgeman Art Library International; (b) Ronald C.

Modra/Sports Imagery/Getty Images. 232: Blaine Harrington III/Corbis. 234: age fotostock / SuperStock. 235: Stephanie Maze/CORBIS. 236: (tcr) Julia Waterlow; Eye Ubiquitous/CORBIS. 237: Andre Vieira/Stringer/Getty Images. 238: Jacques Jangoux / Photo Researchers, Inc. 239: Worldwide Picture Library / Alamy. 240: age fotostock / SuperStock. 242: Russell Gordon/Newscom. 243: (b) Kit Houghton/CORBIS; (r) Tim Brakemeier/Newscom. 244: (t) Bettmann/CORBIS; (b) Fox Photos/Stringer/Getty Images. 245: ALI BURAFI/AFP/Getty Images. 246: Associated Press. 247: GIRAUD PHILIPPE/CORBIS SYGMA. 248: (b) REUTERS/CORBIS; (t) ASSOCIATED PRESS. 249: Reuters/CORBIS. 250: (c) Jeremy Horner/CORBIS. 250-251: (bkgd) Jeremy Horner/CORBIS. 251: (c) Fernando Bengoechea/Beateworks/Corbis. 252: (b) PAUL SUTHERLAND/National Geographic Image Collection; (t) David W. Hamilton/Getty Images. 253: Jochen Schlenker/Masterfile. 256: Nicholas Prior/Getty Images

ACKNOWLEDGMENTS

Grateful acknowledgment is given to the following authors and publishers. Every effort has been made to trace the ownership of all copyrighted material and to secure the necessary permissions to reprint these selections. In the case of some selections for which acknowledgment is not given, extensive research has failed to locate the copyright holders.
Excerpt from "I Have a Dream" reprinted by arrangement with the Estate of Martin Luther King Jr., c/o Writers House as agent for the proprietor New York, NY. Copyright 1963 Martin Luther King Jr., copyright renewed 1991 Coretta Scott King.